WHEN YOU PRESIDE

WHEN YOU PRESIDE

Fifth Edition

Prior Editions by

SIDNEY S. SUTHERLAND

by

John D. Lawson, Ed.D.

Director Emeritus, Activities Planning Center
California Polytechnic State University
San Luis Obispo

The Interstate
PRINTERS & PUBLISHERS, INC.

DANVILLE, ILLINOIS 61832

WHEN YOU PRESIDE

Fifth Edition

Library of Congress Catalog Card No. 78-58208

ISBN 0-8134-2036-9

The inspiration to write this book came from the original author, Sidney S. Sutherland, my friend and associate for many years and my personal and academic advisor at the University of California at Davis as I struggled through the Master's program.

It is also the result of an exciting doctoral experience at Stanford University under the mentor of mentors, H. B. McDaniel, also an associate and admirer of the incomparable Sid Sutherland.

Lastly, I dedicate this book to my students and staff at Cal Poly and the Young Farmers of California with whom, collectively, I have shared the satisfaction and fulfillment of their development through group activities for most of my professional life.

John D. Lawson

Preface

This book is written for my neighbor across the street and for all those thousands of people like her in this country of ours: the men and women who are willing to step forward and take the lead in community, civic, and business affairs. It is written to help people who, like my neighbor, take the time and expend the effort to work for the good of their respective communities; the kind of people who lead women's clubs, service clubs, youth organizations, parent-student-teacher groups, school boards, and planning commissions; the kind of people who belong to and support those many groups that are working for the betterment of our way of life.

It is written, too, for other persons who, as a part of their jobs, must work effectively with people in groups: persons who supervise, lead, and direct; persons who must help the group they lead to think through problems and goals, make decisions, and form plans for constructive action.

There are three parts. The first four chapters (Part 1) place the emphasis on people—the kind you find *in* groups as well as the kind who *lead* groups; an overview of effective group discussions is provided as well as some of the basics on interaction, listening skills, etc. The eight chapters of Part 2 present you with techniques, processes, and "special 'things'" that make a group into a lively and valuable experience for both you and the members of your group. The final chapters form Part 3, a unit designed as a guideline for more formal groups: symposiums, committee meetings, panel discussions, etc. Within this section you'll find "Parliamentary Procedure Made Easy," a chapter that's sure to ease the way for any formal leadership responsibilities that may be on your agenda.

This book has been written to you and for you. If it helps you and your organization, and if it hits the target more often than it misses, my time in writing it and yours in reading it will be time well spent. May it help you—

When *You* Preside.

John D. Lawson

Contents

About the Author

The author of a practical book like WHEN YOU PRESIDE is expected to be an experienced leader himself. John D. Lawson, from Eagle Scout to Commanding Officer of major war vessels of the United States Navy and high school student body president to Dean of Students at a major university with a doctorate in Education from Stanford University, is such an author.

His undergraduate years at the University of California–Berkeley were rich with activities: participating in intercollegiate athletics, the Cal Band, and three student organizations; serving as president of a social fraternity; and receiving leadership honors from the U.S. Naval R.O.T.C. and university intramural sports.

As a young high school teacher of vocational agriculture, his F.F.A. chapter achieved many county fair and state honors with educational exhibits and demonstrations. Judging and parliamentary procedure teams were sources of pride to the entire community.

Captain Lawson's U.S. Navy career was brilliant. His first sea duty as an inexperienced ensign was to command a 110-foot submarine chaser with a crew of 22 equally inexperienced men. By war's end, he had commanded five ships with distinction and had been selected to train other officers in matters of ship organization and personnel motivation and management. His post-war leadership as Battalion Commander of a Naval Reserve training center was cited by the Commandant, Twelfth Naval District.

During his five years as Special Supervisor on the staff of the Bureau of Agricultural Education, Lawson developed the California Young Farmers Association with more than 100 chapters in every region of the state. He established programs for officer training, annual conventions, farm judging, and public speaking and parliamentary procedure contests and a bimonthly newsletter that continues even today. These were the years of close association with Sidney S. Sutherland and the genesis of the first edition of WHEN YOU PRESIDE.

Appointment as Director of the Activities Planning Center at Cal Poly State University, advanced studies in educational and social psychology, group dynamics and organizational development at U.C. Davis and Stanford University opened up a productive environment for new experiences. Nearly 300 campus organizations and governmental and program groups became laboratories for student learning and development in Lawson's psychology classes. Weekends were times for student workshops and retreats. Later, these weekends were extended throughout the state and nation for all sorts of organizations that were eager to send their leaders for personal and social development. These include service clubs, the American Farm Bureau Federation, the Association of College Unions, Girl Scouts, Y.W.C.A., Hotline, California Grange, the American College Personnel Association, the Agricultural Leadership Associates, social fraternities and sororities, and university classes in recreation leadership and teacher education; bookstore managers, college housing directors, and college and university activities advisers.

The Leadership Development Team was established as a partnership in 1976, and the book *Leadership Is Everybody's Business* co-authored by Leslie J. Griffin and Franklyn D. Donant was published by Impact Publishers, Inc., San Luis Obispo, California.

During the years as professor of psychology at Cal Poly, only one text, WHEN YOU PRESIDE, offered a practical approach to group leadership that gave student leaders what they needed, and hundreds of copies moved through the university bookstore into the hands of grateful students. It seems only proper that Professor Lawson would become heir to bringing the Fifth Edition of Sutherland's WHEN YOU PRESIDE into print with his own rich background of studies and experience.

So, You're in Charge

So they're holding a meeting! And you're in charge. Sooner or later it seems to happen to almost everyone—businessmen, housewives, mechanics, farmers, truck drivers, engineers, you, and me.

Maybe you brought it upon yourself. Perhaps there's a problem of management in your firm, and you've called a meeting of your associates to thresh it out. Maybe, like fame, you've earned it. Perhaps your neighbors have elected you to the city council, and the council in turn has selected you as chairperson. Perhaps (also like fame), you've had it thrust upon you. The phone rings and a feminine voice says, "The ladies of the Monday Club want to meet and discuss plans for raising money for the new community swimming pool, and *we want **you** to lead the discussion!*"

America not only is the sweet land of liberty but also the land of meetings—meetings to discuss problems both large and small; meetings to point with pride and to view with alarm; meetings to plan and to review; big meetings and small meetings; formal gatherings and informal ones—and all meetings need leaders to make them successful.

Within the next day or the next week, the next year or the next few hours, the odds are all in favor of your being called upon to take the lead in one of them. So, if you're the kind of a person who's attracted by this title, or a person who has already been tapped for such a job or likely will be soon, perhaps you'd best read and study the book now; then, when you're called upon to take the chair, you'll be ready, and your friends and colleagues will say, "Chris, we knew you could do it."

If you bought the book because you've already stumbled through your first meeting and you want to do better, you're still ahead; first, because you are now aware of some of the problems with presiding and second, because you are probably more motivated than you've ever been before about learning some "surefire" ways to make your meetings *more* human and *more* effective.

Let's assume that you find yourself in charge, looking at a lot of expectant faces belonging to people who are just waiting for something to happen. It's all yours. What are you going to do about it?

For most of us, at least those of us who are not extreme extroverts and who are not automatically the life of every party, greeting those expectant faces and that dead silence at the beginning of every meeting can be an appalling experience—one that sets the butterflies fluttering in our stomachs.

It needn't be painful. It can be fun—fun for you and fun for the group you're leading. But how do you do it so that it will be a pleasure and not an ordeal for you and your associates?

If you read this entire book, you will learn a lot about the finer points of conducting successful group meetings in general. That's why it has been written. But if you'll just read and put into practice the four things that are emphasized in the next few paragraphs, you will have the key to effective group leadership. Read them and try them, and experience for yourself how simple it really is.

1. Become one of the group as quickly as possible. You're already set apart from the group physically by virtue of the fact that you're the leader. That blank silence is a wall between you and the group and between each individual in the group and the person next to him or her. Break it down! Get into it with them. Be informal and at ease. Forget yourself. Don't stand on your dignity; smile, and watch them relax. Become one of the group actually as well as in spirit. If all members are sitting, sit with them. Move as close to them as possible. Get acquainted with them, and get them acquainted with each other. Become identified with them. Effective democratic leadership of a group lies in relinquishing your status and so-called authority as leader as quickly as possible and in getting the members of the group to share this responsibility. Sound like a paradox? Nevertheless, it's true. The quicker you can toss them the ball and have them enjoy the feel of it, the better you'll be functioning as a leader.

Relax them, acquaint them, and put them at ease; get them to take the initiative; become one of them. (To do this, you might try one of the several get-acquainted exercises in *Leadership Is Everybody's Business.*[1])

2. Get them to talk and participate as soon as possible. The surest way to throw a wet blanket on any group discussion, large or small, is for the leader to attempt to start it off with a formal, prepared speech. It doesn't matter how well you do it or how important the things are that you feel compelled to get off your chest, the longer *you* talk, the tougher it will be to get *the rest of them* started.

It seems to be a natural impulse for a leader to want to talk, especially at the start of a meeting. But consider this for a moment. If you're going to do all or most of the talking, why call the meeting at all? If *you* feel the urge to talk, how about the others? Perhaps they'd like to hear themselves, too. So watch that impulse to make a speech, and smother it.

You do want this meeting to be an interesting one, so mark well and remember that participation begets interest; interest begets more participation; more participation begets more interest, which in turn . . . well, even the psychologists don't know which comes first, but they all know that interest is both a *cause* and an *effect* of participation. Just as in the old story of the chicken and the egg, we don't know which comes first, but it doesn't matter. In the poultry business you can start with hens and get eggs; for a successful meeting you can start with participation and get interest. It's just that simple, but many people who should know better don't observe this rule, and the result is just another dull meeting!

---

[1]John D. Lawson, Leslie J. Griffin, Randy D. Donant, *Leadership Is Everybody's Business*, Impact Publishers, Inc., San Luis Obispo, California, 1976.

If you talk longer than it takes to present the group members with an interesting question or problem, or if, as the meeting progresses, you find yourself talking more than 50 percent of the time, regard this as a danger signal. You aren't doing so well as a group leader. *You* may be interested, but are *they?*

So, get the members talking and participating within the first few minutes; they'll love it and you'll *still* be in charge.

3. Give them something to think about. Conducting a meeting and leading a group discussion is nothing more nor less than leading group thinking. If you want people in a group to think, they must be given something to think about. It takes a problem to start people to thinking. Groups do not discuss topics or subjects readily, but they will discuss problems. So either present a problem yourself to start the discussion or ask the members of the group to state the problem that they have come to talk about.

In presenting a problem, state it briefly, clearly, succinctly, and *ask them what they're going to do about it.* Then stay alert but silent and let them solve it; help them out only when they need it.

4. Help them help themselves. This is your major job as a leader. You can begin by relieving the tension at the start of a meeting through creating an informal atmosphere and becoming one of the group. You can continue it by encouraging your co-members to talk and to take part in the discussions. You can foster it by helping them select problems to solve and by stating them clearly. Finally, you can make it possible for them to think these problems through by questioning, by encouraging the quiet ones to talk, by keeping the discussion from straying off the subject, and by making use of all the know-how, all the good judgment, and all the sound reasoning that the 15 or 50 members of this group represent.

Don't do their thinking for them. Help them help themselves. You should be the *last* source of information—literally.

Remember these four things and practice them in conducting informal discussions, formal meetings, panels—any kind of a gathering where you want group participation. These steps are the keys to successful group leadership.

1. Become one of the group as quickly as possible.
2. Get the members to talk and participate as soon as possible.
3. Give them something to think about.
4. Help them help themselves.

Of course, there is more to it than this, and it isn't as simple as it may sound. But as you read WHEN YOU PRESIDE, notice how often these principles will appear as the foundations of the tried and proved procedures for leading groups.

Part

1

The People

*People come in all sorts of shapes, sizes, and adornments. "Viva la difference!" Just looking different, however, is little or nothing when compared with how differently each person **perceives** what is going on. No two of us are perceptually alike simply because no two of us have experienced the same life—from the inside looking out—since the moment of birth. So, after receiving millions of stimuli and bearing the many consequences of our actions, we each become, and remain, a unique person. Since we experience the seeing, feeling, hearing, tasting, and smelling of things uniquely, we have different perceptions of every single thing that happens in the world around us.*

Those of us who find ourselves in leadership positions, whether by election, appointment, or circumstance, would do well to appreciate the power of this complex, but common, human trait. Understanding it will make us more able to help the people in our groups work together toward mutual goals.

*Part 1, therefore, is devoted to a four-chapter discussion of how individual uniqueness operates in groups. By the time you've read it, you should have a working knowledge of how to lead informal group discussions; you'll be introduced to the kind of people you find in groups; you'll study various leadership styles and how they affect others; and you'll know how you can help group members better understand one another through improving the quality of **interpersonal communication.***

1

1

Effective Group Discussions

It has been said that modern life is group life; that the individual who chooses to play the lone wolf and to get results solely through individual effort not only is becoming a rarity but also, in many ways, a socially handicapped person.

Two heads are better than 1, and 10 heads are better than 2, especially in finding the solutions and the answers to social problems. Sometimes a skilled person may solve a technical difficulty in business, engineering, or agriculture more effectively unaided than through group action. Research has shown, however, that even in non-social problems, group thinking can be more effective than individual effort. Besides, this is a democracy, and group thinking is the foundation of democracy and an important (if not essential) factor in its functioning. One advocate of democratic discussion put it this way:

> If persons would do what they are told, and if leaders could agree as to what they should be told, we might dispense with this democratic process of deliberation and simply employ a few experts to tell the rest of us what to do on personal, racial, international, and other questions. When once started on a venture in democracy, however, people demand a right to form their own judgments on the basis of evidence. The only way to insure the future of democracy is to secure such experience in this process that people will become able to make increasingly better decisions.

3

To bring it closer to home, the everyday problems within communities and neighborhoods are being more and more frequently settled from action started by discussing these problems in small groups. Should there be a zoning problem confronting the City Planning Commission, the people directly involved are called together to talk it over. The need for a summer recreation program is vaguely sensed by people in general, but the planning is turned over to a small group of representatives from interested organizations.

Conferences, conventions, workshops, and most meetings involving large numbers of people eventually break down into small discussion groups where the real thinking is done and where decisions are made. In national and in state government as well as in large organizations of any kind, the bulk of the work is done by committees.

So it takes many kinds of small group meetings: formal committees assigned specific problems and informal groups getting together just to talk things over, to make things go, to keep them going, and to make possible our modern and democratic way of life.

Now, what does it take to make these groups function effectively? Who does what to make them function? What are the earmarks of good group discussions?

The earmarks of a good discussion and a good group are these:

1. *A good group discussion is informal.* Everyone is at ease, spirits are high, there is friendly disagreement, and everyone has a good time.

2. *Everyone participates* and the discussion is scattered among all members. No one dominates. All profit from the experiences of others.

3. *It accomplishes something,* in that the group arrives at decisions as to what to do or what not to do.

4. *It creates a "we" spirit and attitude,* welding a number of individuals into a group with a common purpose. It fosters a feeling of belonging and of cooperation.

5. *It stimulates thinking* and encourages each member to do individual thinking on problems common to all members of the group.

6. *The members are interested* in the problem under discussion, in the meeting itself, and in the interchange of ideas; and they cooperate to make it a success.

7. *It checks up on itself,* objectively examining how well the group and the individual members are working, cooperating, and progressing.

The preceding things happen when we have effective group dynamics, and hence, a good meeting; this is the end product we're after. But *who* does *what* to make it all happen? In its simplest form, it takes only a leader and a group in which leadership roles emerge among the members. Many group discussions are conducted totally with just a leader and a recorder. But as problems multiply, and as occasion demands, other roles may be added. From this point it can grow into a full-fledged leadership team with a designated leader, a recorder, an observer, a consultant, and other various group members. The varied duties for each of these roles are described more fully at the end of this chapter. But for now, let's take a look at the skills involved in developing an effective democratic leadership role.

The Effective Leader

Important as your role is in leading an informal group discussion, the fewer things you have to do as a leader after the discussion starts, the more effective you will be. The chances are that the group you will be leading will be made up of a dozen of your neighbors, associates, and friends, people who know something about the subject under discussion and who have common problems they want to work out together. They have met to learn together, to exchange and pool experiences—not to be instructed by you.

Let's discuss what you should do *before, beginning,* and *during* the meeting.

Before the Meeting

1. Be there ahead of time—before others get there if possible.

2. Arrange the room so that the setting is right. Be your own expediter. See that the room is neither too hot nor too cold, that there is good light, that there is a chalkboard or newsprint pad and easel available, that *your* chair is located where it ought to be, and that the rest of the chairs are arranged satisfactorily.

3. Take a few moments to review mentally what you are going to do and how you are going to start the discussion. Jot down a few notes if you wish, such as:

    a. Your opening remarks.

    b. A clear-cut brief statement of the problem.

    c. Some pertinent facts regarding the problem (to be used only if necessary to supplement those supplied by the group).

    d. Some possible conclusions or solutions.

4. Always remember the four commandments for leading discussion groups:

Become and remain one of them.

Help them talk and work together.

Give them something to think about.

Help them help themselves.

5. As the others arrive, greet them and treat them as though they were visitors to your home. Chat with them, relax, be one of them, and introduce those who may be strangers.

Beginning the Meeting

1. Make a *brief* introductory statement of the purpose of the meeting.

2. Get acquainted with your group and introduce the members to each other if necessary. Use the methods discussed in Chapter 6.

3. State the problem that they have met to discuss and solve. State it in the form of a question. Define and clarify it yourself, or:

4. Have them do it. Ask, "Just exactly what do we want to accomplish? What do we want to have happen? What's the best possible outcome?"

5. Ask for tentative or possible solutions. Get as many as possible.

During the Meeting

1. Call for facts and arguments for and against each possible solution.

2. Keep the discussion centered on the problem and on the track.

3. Stimulate and encourage participation by everyone.

4. Summarize when necessary and contribute facts when called for; but resist that impulse to do the thinking and talking for everyone.

5. Make sure every possible solution has a hearing and is fairly weighed, evaluated, and discussed.

6. When agreement has been reached on the best answer or answers, make a brief final summary, and bring the meeting to a close or proceed to a new problem.

The procedure outlined is typical of the discussion centering around a problem stated by you as a leader. However, as it quite frequently happens, you as a leader may suggest only a subject or topic and draw out the problem from the group.

When this happens your procedure in opening the meeting is different in that you lead the group to decide upon and state the problem as well as to define and clarify it.

Special Competencies for the Leader

The following methods should be a part of every discussion leader's repertoire. Their effective use may well make the difference between a really worthwhile discussion and one that hits the rock bottom of utter boredom for everyone and stays there.

● *Questioning.* Two general types of questions should be included in your repertoire: the so-called *overhead* or *general type* of question and the *direct* question. The overhead question often calls for a "yes" or "no" answer. It is directed to the group as a whole and is often used to point out or suggest a line of thought or a possible answer. Some examples are:

"Can we expect people generally to be enthusiastic about a program which will increase their taxes?"

"Should we always try to get absolute perfection?"

The overhead question is also used at the beginning of a discussion. In this case, it may be a statement of the main problem and is directed to the group as a whole. In this case it probably will not be a question answerable by "yes" or "no" and does not suggest a line of thought.

The direct question is usually directed to an individual in the group. This type of question may be used to draw out the timid person who isn't contributing; to secure information about the point under discussion; or to bring a scattered, wandering discussion back to the point.

In using this kind of a question, keep these things in mind:

1. State the question first, wait for someone to respond, or name the person whom you wish to hear from. Never state the name first and then the question, for two obvious reasons: You'll scare the timid and no one but the person named will listen to the question.

2. Use questions beginning with "why," "how," and "which" rather than with "what." "What" calls for a factual answer only, not for thought. Ask "what" only when you're digging for facts.

3. Generally avoid leading questions that suggest their own answers.

4. Give everyone time to think when you ask a question. Don't be in a hurry to get an answer, and don't be afraid of the silence. If people are silent, they're thinking, and that's what you want. So, after every question, pause . . . don't hurry them . . . then recognize the person you want to respond to the question by giving that person a nod or a cue.

● *Turning questions back to the group.* If you answer a question asked by a member of the group, you automatically stop discussion—at least inhibit it rather than encourage it. Therefore, when you are asked a question, refer it to the group as a whole or to some member of the group rather than answer it yourself. Your job is to stimulate discussion. So, when a member asks a question and directs it seemingly to you as a leader, simply turn it back to the group as an overhead question to all or to some one person who indicates that he or she may have something to say about it. Only if no one has any ideas or any answers should *you* undertake an answer.

● *Keeping arguments balanced.* This is the most important skill for those who would become really skillful in leading a group discussion. When you have mastered this technique, you will have crossed the line which separates the good from the ordinary.

There are at least two sides to every question, sometimes more, and it is your duty as a discussion leader to see that each side has a fair hearing. Furthermore, a discussion never gets very interesting until some controversy arises. Here is an example of the way to aid in creating a controversy and then keeping it under control:

Suppose you're having a meeting of the parents of children in a neighborhood club. You raise the question, "Do you think we ought to plan a parents' work day to clean up the grounds around the park and do some needed repair work on the building itself?" Now, if you let nature take its course after asking a question like that, here's what probably will happen.

Some parent will come up with a statement that goes something like this:

I think we should. The building is in pretty bad shape. The roof leaks; there's hardly a window in the place that isn't broken; there's no place to store projects that the children are working on; and the wiring needs overhauling. The yard is a mess. The weeds are over a foot high; the shrubs need pruning; there ought to be a new flag pole put up. Why, there're all kinds of jobs that need doing that we can do. I don't think there's any question about it. We ought to organize a work day, get everybody out, and give both the building and the park a thorough going over. I say we ought to get at it.

Now, as a leader, where do you go from there? You have an answer to your question, and you have a lot of reasons for one side of that question. Now, how are you going to bring out the other side in the face of such an impressive array of sustaining evidence? It would take a pretty hardy soul, wouldn't it, to take issue with the responses that were given? As a result, either your discussion will die right there, or else, after a lot of pumping from you, you might get someone to present the other side of the question and some reasons why a work day might not be the thing.

Yes, something went wrong. This is what happened and what you should prevent. You asked a question and then allowed one person to give one side of the question and *reasons* in detail *before* you found out what the opinions were of *every* member of the group. As a result, the negative answer never had a hearing, and it is reasonable to assume that not everyone was immediately enthusiastic about the prospect of a parents' work day.

Suppose, instead, you had handled it another way. After you raised the overhead question, "Do you think we should plan a parents' work day, etc?," you added another question, "What does each of you think about that? Don't give any reasons, yet, but just your immediate opinion."

You very quickly get an answer from everyone. Then, asking for a show of hands, you find that of the 16 parents, 9 seem to favor a work day and 7 don't. You select one of the minority opinion-holders and ask for these reasons. Then one of the proponents of the work day speaks up and states the case for cleaning up the building and park. (It will be done now because the majority is most likely to be supported.) Now, another of the minority comes to the aid of the first speaker—and—you've got a good discussion going. Furthermore, you're seeing to it that *both* sides of the question have a hearing.

Here, in brief, is the procedure you should follow to get a spirited discussion of an overhead question or a problem, and to make sure that all phases of the problem and all sides of the question have a hearing and are considered.

1. State the problem or overhead question. Give everyone a moment to think it over.

2. Call for answers or opinions without reasons.

3. Get everyone on record as to his or her tentative or immediate opinion regarding the question.

4. Call for one or more of the minority opinion-holders to give reasons for his or her position. If everyone fails to make a good case, offer help by means of questions which point toward arguments that may have been overlooked.

5. Ask for reasons from the majority group or allow them to state their case. Strengthen their arguments if necessary by questions which will open up new points in favor of this opinion.

6. Let nature take its course; let proponents of both sides continue the discussion, but break in when necessary with questions designed to strengthen whichever case seems to need it at that moment. Do not reveal which side you favor by anything you say or do or by your facial expression.

7. When, and only when, both sides have had ample opportunity to defend their stands, and when you have made sure that all phases of the question have been explored, either allow the stronger side to convince the minority or arrive at a satisfactory compromise. Generally, if there is a right answer or one conclusion which is markedly better, the group will arrive at it unaided.

8. If it does not, summarize the reasons pro and con, then:

Ask for a compromise.

Form a committee.

> Call for a recess to get together with "key"
> advocates to reach a compromise.
> Vote.

Suspense is one of the most potent methods of arousing and maintaining interest. Inviting competition is another. This procedure involves both of these strong human dynamics.

In finding out how everyone stands on the question, avoid if possible asking for a show of hands—a vote. Instead, ask for two volunteers: one to present the reasons why the project should be done and another to give reasons why it should not be done. If these two do a thorough job, ask for a show of hands in support of one, then the other. If, in your judgment, there is more that should be brought out, ask, "Would anyone else like to add a point on one side or the other?," then ask for the vote. This is likely to get all the affirmative and all the negative points out in the open with a minimum of risk that anyone would dominate the discussion. Then simply ask how many agree and how many disagree. If they choose to indicate their agreement by raising their hands, all right, but don't ask them to do it.

Another way to get both sides out early is to brainstorm both sides of the issue openly and as described in Chapter 10.

● *Using a "problem checklist."* While a group usually meets to discuss a specific problem pretty much agreed upon beforehand, sometimes just a general topic is suggested, and it is the duty of the group to select the problem it wishes to discuss. In a situation of this kind, the *response* to the leader's question, "Well, just what problems do we want to discuss tonight?," might be just a little disappointing. No one, or at least very few, may be prepared to voice a clear idea.

To avoid this, prepare a list of possible problems which you feel these people might wish to discuss, and have it duplicated. See that all have a copy and ask that each one checks the one, two, or three which he or she would like to have discussed. After all have done this, take a poll and use the problem in which there was evidently the most interest. See Chapter 8 for an example and additional uses of this technique.

● *Curbing the over-talkative person.* This, of course, is our old friend the "monopolizer" or "table-thumper." Ignore such people if you can; don't see or hear their efforts to get the floor; don't let them catch your eye. Instead, give your attention to anyone else who indicates a desire to speak. If they *won't* be ignored; if one gets wound up and well under way, your only recourse may be to forget that you're a gentleman or a lady and simply interrupt; give a compliment for the contribution, and ask someone else to take it from there.

● *Encouraging the shy person.* One of your main jobs as a leader is to see that everyone takes part. You'll always have those who would rather listen than talk. Keep your eyes open for them and as you spot them, encourage them to take part. For example, when someone has made a statement, ask, "What do you think of that statement, Charlie?" Do you agree or disagree?," or, "Do you have anything to add to that statement, Carol?"

● *Handling the sorehead, the argumentative person.* Refuse to be drawn into an argument. Make this a hard and fast rule and stick to it. Don't try to convince him or her. Your success won't be and isn't measured by your ability to get 100 percent agreement, so don't worry if someone doesn't agree and aggressively says so. Ignore the person and ease the tension with a joke or a statement (and a smile) that you're not going to try to convince or argue. Usually the others will support you.

● *Bringing the group to a decision.* Too often discussions don't seem to get anywhere. There is a good discussion of the problem, but it goes on and on and no decision is reached. It is the duty of the leader, of course, to see that this doesn't happen. Here is where the role of *summarizer* is played to help the group arrive at an agreement as to the best solution to the problem under discussion. There are a number of ways this can be done. Sometimes a discussion can be concluded by "general consent," saying, "Well, on the basis of what we've discussed, it seems that most of us feel . . ." It may be necessary to restate the arguments for and against the proposal under consideration and call for a motion and a vote. This should only be done, however, as the last resort.

One of the better ways, and a method which will help the group to weigh the facts and arrive at its own conclusions follows. It consists of the leader's asking the group to apply a three-way test to each solution suggested and on the basis of this test arrive at a conclusion. The following involves overhead questions to be presented by the leader.

1. Will this solution accomplish what we want to have happen?
   (Will it attain our major purposes?)
2. Can it be done?
3. Do the facts justify it?
   (What facts support it? Which are in conflict with it?)

This test applied to each of the stands or solutions proposed by the group will generally indicate which is the best.

In summary, these things characterize a good discussion and effective democratic leadership:

1. It is informal. The leader establishes and sustains this kind of an atmosphere.

2. Everyone participates. The leader makes it a point to see that everyone does participate and that he or she doesn't monopolize the discussion.

3. A cooperative attitude is maintained.

4. It stimulates thinking. The leader presents problem situations, brings out all pertinent facts, keeps the arguments balanced, and brings the group to a definite conclusion.

5. It accomplishes something. Decisions are made.

6. The members are interested. The leader creates and maintains suspense, using interesting procedures.

7. It checks up on itself. It makes use of either an official or an unofficial observer.

The following section is designed to give you an idea of some of the *roles* that can emerge within a group, their corresponding duties, and how these compare with the responsibilities of the leader and group members.

The Leader

Helps the members get acquainted with one another.

Establishes and maintains an informal atmosphere.

States the problem or helps the group state it.

Stimulates and directs the discussion toward the solution of the problem; keeps it moving.

Promotes participation by all members.

Notes contributions of members on chalkboard or chart.

Encourages the timid; discourages the monopolizer.

Stimulates thinking; sees that all sides of the question are heard.

Helps the group check up on itself by using and assisting the recorder and observer.

Stays in the background; avoids imposing his or her own views on the group.

Summarizes when necessary.

Brings the group to a conclusion and helps it develop a plan of action.

The Recorder

Keeps a record of the main problems, facts, and decisions brought out in the discussion.

Summarizes and reports at the end of the session or at the beginning of the next.

Summarizes discussion from time to time when requested.

Prepares a final group report.

The Observer

Pays special attention to how the group and its leaders operate and progress.

Checks on the amount and kind of participation by members.

Checks on the effectiveness of the leader.

Checks on the thinking and the attitude of the group.

Reports to the group what he or she has observed from time to time, during the meeting and at the close.

The Consultant

Supplies information and facts at the request of the group or leader.

Cites experiences at request or when it is appropriate to the discussion.

Assists leader in seeing that all pertinent facts are considered.

Assists leader in keeping the group moving toward decisions and solutions.

The Group Member

Contributes ideas and suggestions pertaining to the problem.

Assumes various leadership roles as the need arises.

Gives the group the benefit of personal experience.

Listens to what others say and respects their contributions.

Keeps "on the subject" with all comments.

Avoids both of the two extremes, monopolizing the discussion and saying nothing.

Cooperates with the group to solve a common problem.

Keeps prejudices and personal aims from causing undue influence.

Works with other members to help the group to progress and become a unit.

In Chapter 2, the realm of individual roles is more fully explored.

2

The People in Groups

The most effective meetings are those that involve many people. And it is a part of your job as a leader to recognize the potential within the membership, to use it, to direct it into useful channels, and to harness it in such a way that it will bring people together rather than force them apart. For there is always a tremendous amount of varied leadership in any group. To do this you must first know how this leadership may be expressed and be able to identify the various forms it may take.

Just as "all the world's a stage, and all the men and women merely players," so each group has its unique cast. Some of the cast are heroes, some are villains; some seek the spotlight, others avoid it; some have speaking parts, others manage the props. But unlike in the theater, in groups, no one assigns these roles; each player simply assumes the one that fits his or her own needs and personality best.

Do you know someone who invariably is elected secretary of every organization to which he or she belongs? Probably you do, for there are many people who find themselves in this and similar situations. That's their way of expressing their need to play a leadership role. They keep the written records of the matters discussed and of the decisions made. They are the unsung heroes of many successful organizations.

In contrast, do you happen to know some person who seems

always to be "anti" everything? Unfortunately, you probably know one of these, too, for there seems to be one or more in almost every group. These are the villians in groups, the bad guys.

You can also expect to find people in your meetings who naturally assume roles that are helpful. There will be others (but happily not as many) who hinder, work against, and detract from the work of the group. Let's consider the helpful types first.

Dr. D. M. Hall in his book, *Dynamics of Group Action*, published by The Interstate Printers & Publishers, Inc., identifies and describes at least 14 *roles* which he states must be played by the members of any group if effective group discussion and action are to occur. I'm sure you'll recognize most of them, and we've borrowed quite a bit from Dr. Hall's descriptions in the following paragraphs. Here goes:

1. The Initiator. The person who's always starting something—bringing up a new problem, suggesting a new activity, proposing a new plan for the group to discuss. Generally, the leader must play this role, but it's nice to have several initiators in the group to help out, people who have the initiative and the imagination to sense problems, and to clarify, define, and state them so that they present a challenge to the other members. Encourage any member who shows even a trace of this tendency!

2. The Orientator. The person who's likely to ask, "Now, just what is our problem? What is it we're trying to accomplish?" He or she helps focus the thinking and the discussion of the group on the problem at hand and serves to keep everyone on the right track. This is a role which the good leader must be prepared to play, but if you're lucky, there may be another "orientator" in the group. If you note this, back off, let it happen, and thank the person!

3. The Facilitator. The person who keeps the pot boiling and the discussion going, generally by asking questions like, "Now, Mary, you said you were opposed to a door-to-door canvass to raise funds. Would you explain it?" or, "Sam, I didn't get exactly what you were driving at in that last statement; would you repeat it and make it a little clearer?" A facilitator is a kind of catalyst for a good discussion; a couple of uninhibited facilitators in your group will take a big load off your shoulders as the presiding officer.

4. The Encourager. This is the member who stimulates others to greater activity by showing approval and giving encouragement. An encourager smiles, nods, pantomimes a hand clap, or holds a hand up with thumb and finger forming the well-known "OK" sign whenever someone makes a helpful statement. Doesn't it give you a nice, warm feeling when you've made a statement and an enthusiastic "encourager" gives you the high sign that says, "You tell 'em. Those're my sentiments, too."?

5. The Harmonizer. This person is the smoother-outer, the really mature person who makes a rational attempt to have all sides of the question considered, realizing that progress is based on differences of opinion and that debate must occur in any spirited discussion. The harmonizer often saves the day and reduces tension by a pointed or humorous story or quip. Be thankful if there's a harmonizer in your group, and be prepared to *be one* if there isn't.

As indicated earlier, these are parts that a leader must be prepared to play, but only if they are not assumed by other members of the group. An effective leader relinquishes leadership as others are able to handle it, so as soon as an *initiator*, an *orientator*, a *facilitator*, an *encourager*, or a *harmonizer* surfaces, be encouraging, and assist in the specific role's development.

The next few roles are *not* generally within the province of the presiding officer, but you might have to accept some of these responsibilities from time to time under certain conditions.

6. *The Recorder*. The recorder keeps a written record of the decisions and the actions of the group and reports them to the group members or to the public. The secretary who keeps the minutes of a formal meeting is a recorder. This is generally recognized as an essential leadership role, and someone is usually designated to perform this function as soon as a group is organized.

7. *The Evaluator*. This is the person in the group who tries to determine the progress the group is making toward its objectives. When the discussion seems to be bogged down or going around in circles, the evaluator is likely to speak up and say, "Well, we don't seem to be getting anywhere this way; let's see whether this other approach will help." Or, when things *are* going well, "We seem to have pretty well decided that the first alternative is the way to go." This role is closely related to and is often combined with—

8. *The Analyzer.* The analyzer takes notes and perhaps even records the extent to which each member of the group is participating and contributing to the solution of the problem under discussion. The analyzer may keep track of the progress of the group as a whole, may take note of the way in which members are cooperating or failing to cooperate in working toward a common objective, or he or she may chart the effectiveness of the presiding officer in directing and guiding the group. Often this person is the third member of a team consisting of the presiding officer, the recorder, and the evaluator-analyzer, each of whom has such a well-defined part to play that it is officially recognized and designated.

9. *The Summarizer.* The summarizer is the person who brings together ideas contributed by other members, who points out ideas' relationships to each other, and who suggests a course of action. One person, who is a confirmed "meeting-goer" (a member of the board of regents of a midwestern university and an active member of numerous business, civic, and social organizations), has this to say of the summarizer:

"If I could pick my role in a meeting, that's the one I'd want to be! I know lots of them and I envy them their ability to just lean back after everyone has spoken and come up with something like this, 'Now, John gave us a lot of good facts about the need for equipment for the Boy Scout camp, and I agree with what Tom said about wanting our troop to be the best in the district. I can't go along with Al entirely when he says this is the worst troop in town, but I do agree that it isn't the best by a long shot. So why don't we just each contribute five bucks and ask the other dads to do the same and buy 'em the equipment they need.' When he says that, all the rest begin to nod their heads in agreement and the whole thing is settled. If I could have my choice of group roles, I'd want to be a summarizer."

That's what a summarizer does, boils everything down to its essentials and suggests appropriate action. It's a real leadership role, and every group needs one. Furthermore, this is a part which the presiding officer should not have to play if the group is functioning as it should.

10. The Helper. The helper is primarily concerned with the comfort of the individual members, with the adequacy of the physical setting, and with the materials needed for the meeting. The helper distributes paper and pencils when there is writing to do, finds a chair for the late-comer, opens a window, and adjusts the shades if the sun is shining in someone's eyes. Generally, the helper is an energetic, detail-concerned person who takes pride in assuring that the materials and the human atmosphere that make a meeting go well are available.

11. The Fact-Seeker. Whenever a problem is under discussion, this is the person who offers some statement like, "I don't think we have enough data on which to base a decision. I'd like a few more facts before I decide." This calls for a pretty straight thinker and is an important role, since, in the heat of discussion, *opinions* are apt to be more freely given and considered than are the basic facts of the case. The fact-seeker calls attention to the importance of paying attention to the realities of the situation, and this helps the group to arrive at a sound decision.

12. The Fact-Giver. The fact-giver is the one who cites facts which bear upon the problem under consideration from personal experience or from authority. If the subject being discussed is raising school taxes, this is the person who gives the tax rates for all the other districts in the county, compares them to the local rate, and calls attention to whether the local tax rate is too high or too low. Since facts are almost always necessary to problem-solving discussions, the importance of this role cannot be over-estimated.

13. The Status-Giver. This is the person who is invited and encouraged to become a member of the group because his or her accomplishments, position, attitudes, and abilities are known and respected, not only by members of the group, but also by the general public. We generally notice status-givers operating in larger groups. Having the president of the university, the mayor, or the celebrity greet the assembly and welcome them is just about as essential and as standard at any large convention meeting as the registration desk.

14. The Compromiser. The compromiser is the person who admits that there may be two sides to the argument, and who is willing to give ground in order for progress to be made. Like the harmonizer, it takes a mature person in every respect to appreciate the importance of the compromiser in group processes to personally play this role.

These 14 are the most important and most *desirable* roles that should emerge during group processes. As we hinted at the beginning of this chapter, however, not all the roles that surface when people gather together to thresh out common problems are desirable. The roles described above are primarily democratic roles—normal reactions of persons working together for a common objective. In contrast to these, there are certain autocratic and dominative roles—roles which are primarily selfish. Dr. Hall identifies *eight selfish or dominative role-types.* Watch for these characters; they can cause you trouble as the presiding officer and can be very annoying to the working members of any group.

1. The Distracter. The person in this role appears in many guises. The distracter might bring the morning paper to the meeting and busily pursue his or her favorite section. While the presiding officer is trying to get the meeting under way, the distracter yaks about the latest sports event, the stock market, an academy award movie, or scandal. He or she ridicules everything, writes notes or makes sketches, passes them around, tries to draw attention to himself or herself, and shows a lack of interest in the objective of the group by horseplay or cynicism. The distracter refuses to do his or her part and tries to prevent others from doing theirs.

2. The Aggressor. The aggressor is a tyrant who is always putting others down, while trying to control the meeting, the resources of the group, and other people. This person must win at any cost, and doesn't hesitate to ignore, intimidate, or criticize others. This type will push pet projects through (somehow) and get them done through manipulating a few members. Although most aggressors make a lot of noise and are easily identified, some are pretty foxy and do their evil deeds behind the scenes. Be alert for these occasional destroyers of democratic action and deal with them, if you can, between meetings.

3. The Monopolizer. The monopolizer is a loose-lipped, long-winded character who starts out to ask a simple question and prefaces it with a 5,000-word statement that wanders all over the map and has little or nothing to do with the problem under discussion. He or she can be counted upon to speak up at every opportunity, even interrupting others to do it, rambling on and on *ad nauseam* and *ad infinitum*. When 10 words can be used to do the work of 1, this uninhibited extrovert who just loves to talk will indulge this passion. The monopolizer is a close relative to—

4. The Recognition-Seeker. The recognition-seeker is one who knows all the answers and knows all the important people who know all the answers which he or she doesn't. He or she has done everything and has done it well; knows how to run the government, solve the latest crisis, design the county park, or predict the weather. The recognition-seeker says, "The Governor and I are just like that," or "Be sure my name is listed first on the program and spelled

right!" This person expects and demands special consideration for all his or her statements and positions and shows it by the manner in which his or her pronouncements are made.

5. The Blocker. The blocker is the person who is anti-everything. There is usually no good reason for this negative attitude, but invariably the blocker opposes everything that the majority of the members favor.

6. The Wanderer. The person who is congenitally unable to keep his mind on the subject under discussion or to think consecutively for more than two or three minutes is the wanderer. Just when everyone else is enthusiastically discussing ways and means of raising funds for the community swimming pool, this person pops up with a question or statement regarding the mating habits of sea turtles in the Pacific or some other subject equally remote.

7. The Whisperer. The whisperer is probably a sub-species of the distracter or the recognition-seeker whose specialty is starting a whispering conference with those close by to the confusion of the presiding officer and the discomfort of the rest of the group. Rarely, if ever, does this person contribute to the group as a whole.

8. The Zipper-Mouth. The zipper-mouth just won't talk. He or she sits like the proverbial bump on a log and listens, doesn't disturb anyone, but doesn't contribute either. He or she is indifferent and doesn't seem to want to be bothered with making decisions or getting involved. Probably this person is just shy and perhaps needs to be in a smaller group with a less threatening atmosphere.

These are some, but probably not all, of the troublesome people-types in groups. We hope they won't be in your group, but if they are, be prepared to deal with them. You will find some pointers about how to do this in Chapter 1.

Several of these leadership roles are persistent enough to have been recognized for a long time. The initiator-harmonizer-orientator-facilitator acts as the *leader* of the group. The recorder is generally the secretary who keeps the written records of the deliberations. These you know and are familiar with.

The trend, however, is to expand this team to include many instead of two. Quite often a member may be particularly well-informed on the subject under discussion, and his or her facts may be needed by the group in order to reach a sound conclusion. Such a person may be invited to take part because of this. In this way, the role of "fact-giver" may be expanded into that of the *consultant* who supplies facts and acts as an additional member of the leadership team. Sometimes the consultant is called a "resource-person."

Groups don't always proceed in a straight line toward their objective. They often wander down inviting by-ways instead. Sometimes, in spite of the efforts of the presiding officer, all do not participate. Therefore, the role of "evaluator" and "analyzer" is often combined and added to the leadership team as the observer who helps analyze and evaluate progress.

The functions of each of these people will be described more thoroughly as we go along, but the modern leadership team is made up of more and more people who play helping roles.

3

Leadership Styles

Do you have what it takes to do an effective leadership job with your organization? How is that leadership expressed? What effect does your style of leadership have on the people around you? There are at least four all-too-familiar types of leaders who can be found in almost any business or organization and who fail, in one way or another, to get the most out of the membership. These will be described in the following pages, along with the characteristics of a really democratic leader.

1. The Absolute Dictator, whom we shall call "Abdic," is generally a very able person with a strong opinion about what ought to be done and how to do it. Possibly "Abdic" has built up the business, department, or organization from the start with no help at all. Since at one time "Abdic" alone made all decisions, it is difficult (if not impossible) for this person to delegate or share decision making now. Or maybe "Abdic" has had failures in the past which were blamed on others, thus resulting in a continuing lack of trust in others. Whatever the reason, all decisions are now made by "Number One," and nothing important is done by others without "Abdic's" personal permission. Delegation of authority is definitely out. "Ab-

dic" aggressively cracks the whip, orders people around, sets the policies and procedures, and enforces them harshly. Nonconformers are disciplined publicly, quietly penalized, and even "frozen-out" of the organization in one way or another.

"Abdic" calls meetings, announces the agenda one item at a time, elaborates on the problem, explains the best solution, and announces who is to do what and when he or she is to do it; asks if there are any questions, and hearing none (One can't hear if one doesn't listen!), moves along to the next item on the agenda . . . and so on *adapathium.*

The results of an absolute dictatorship are many—all bad. Some people feel left out, put down, unworthy, and apathetic; others become irritated, frustrated, and angry. Whatever the feelings, you can predict that there will be very little real support from an uninvolved audience except on the part of those few who may be motivated by loyalty to the organization, fear for their future, or the hope of reward.

It is a well-known fact that we are more likely to participate in the hard work that leads to completing a project if we have been involved in deciding what that project is to be. It is also clear that projects and the solutions to problems have greater promise of achieving excellence when they come from the input of many thinking people sharpening their wits on one another than from the idea of one person (or even a group in which all members think alike). Our friend "Abdic," then, is destined to work alone or with a few loyal, fearful, or hopeful followers on projects somewhere below the level of excellence.

2. The Benevolent Leader, whom we will call "Benlead," is dominated by a love of all people and a need to be a "nice guy" to everyone all the time. Members are fond of "Benlead" because their ideas and work are appreciated and praised publicly and profusely. The group seems like one big happy family in which every idea or need is immediately adopted or attended to by "Benlead." In contrast to "Abdic's" absolute dictatorship style of constantly *initiating* ideas and projects, "Benlead" simply *responds* to the thoughts and goals of others. "Whatever they want is probably the best way to proceed since my job is to help satisfy the needs and wishes of others," would probably be "Benlead's" way of expressing his viewpoint. And "Benlead" would step right in and do more than an equal share of the work, too. In fact, *someone* has to do the behind-the-scenes, unpopular "dirty-work" of every project, and since the goal of this leadership style is to keep everyone else happy, "Benlead" would be willing to do it all alone.

"Benlead" calls meetings whenever anyone wants a meeting, requests items for the agenda, lets people talk whenever and as long as they want, uses little or no parliamentary procedure, and turns the meeting over to others whenever anyone wants to assume the leadership role for a while. "Benlead" sets himself or herself up for all the trouble-makers described in Chapter 2—the distracter, aggressor, monopolizer, recognition-seeker, blocker, and wanderer—and they often take advantage of the situation.

The results of benevolent leadership are lack of decisiveness, lack of direction, and lack of progress. A membership or staff of co-workers may enjoy the freedom to do their own thing once in a while, but a daily diet of your favorite dessert can destroy your taste for it. Yes, people do like to be involved in the management of their organization, but they want and expect some balance and direction, too. A year of "Benlead" as presiding officer will be a year of little achievement and one of limited fulfillment for most of the members.

3. The Unpredictable Leader, or "Unpred" for short, is a moody leader who may be an absolute dictator one day and a benevolent one the next, depending on all sorts of external factors. On Monday, if the weekend was OK, "Unpred" might very well be amiable and cheerful, calling others by their nicknames and doing courteous things to make them feel comfortable and secure. "Good morning, Jimmy, have a nice weekend? Good! And how are the wife and kids? That's fine. Why don't we have a cup of coffee before you start work, I'd like to hear about your vacation plans."

Later in the week, when the production reports are in and a terse memorandum from the general manager singled out "Unpred's" department as an example of low efficiency, sweet old "Unpred" transforms from sweet to sour. "James Nauls, I'd like to see you in my office . . . right now! Do you see this production record of my department? I rank lowest of all! You've let me down, and I want to see some changes made, do you hear me? And you might start with a little less time on your coffee breaks!"

"Unpred" is a difficult person to work with. You never know for certain what today's mood will be until there is a display of either "Remember who's boss around here!" or "How was your tennis game over the weekend?" Members in "Unpred's" club or workers in his or her production plant exist in an atmosphere of uncertainty. Much of their time and attention is spent analyzing the mood of the leader or supervisor in order to respond appropriately and avoid trouble. This organization is not likely to have an outstanding year.

4. The Responsibility Avoider ("Resvoid") generally lacks self-confidence and is content to let the organization just drift along instead of choosing to be involved in any meaningful way. Traditional activities and practices continue along as they have in the past with no particular effort or direction from "Resvoid." "If I tried something new, it probably wouldn't work, and the membership wouldn't support it, so why try?" Making decisions is especially threatening so "Resvoid" puts them off as long as possible; "Maybe the problem will solve itself." "Resvoid" was probably elected president during a meeting while absent—or perhaps while grabbing a few quick zzz's in the back row at the time the votes were cast.

The members of any viable organization will resent this style of leadership behavior and will take steps to work around "Resvoid." Splinter groups with their own leaders will often emerge within the membership to keep things going or to do their own thing. Marginal members will lose interest and eventually drop out.

It is not uncommon to have a few "Resvoids" somewhere in the membership. They certainly do not contribute to the vitality and productivity of the organization. But to have a "Resvoid" as president is a year down the drain, a total disaster.

5. The Democratic Leader ("Demy") listens to members and associates, involves them in decision making, and keeps everyone informed of what's going on. At the same time there is no doubt about the importance and responsibility of taking the initiative personally in seeing that the job gets done.

"Demy" is successful in *sharing* problems and decisions with the group and is developing in others a sense of responsibility for their part in the organization. Suggestions are welcomed, and initiative in the development of new projects and procedures is encouraged. "Demy" praises members publicly and, when necessary, "levels" with individuals privately to give constructive criticism. Neither a pat on the back nor a kick in the pants is treated as a personal matter.

Building teamwork (see Chapter 7) is important to "Demy," who never jumps right in on a problem without some positive comments to the group about the progress so far and optimism for the future.

Members under "Demy's" leadership generally exhibit a spirit of fellowship toward one another and an attitude of "pride" and "ownership" in the organization. Projects are *their* projects; successes are *their* successes; and, yes, problems along the way are *their* problems, too. When someone on the team is unable to carry out a specific responsibility, someone else "picks up the slack" (helps without hesitation). All goes well whether "Demy" is physically present or not.

These five examples may be a little extreme, but we've all witnessed a measure of all these traits in people we've known in groups. No one is perfect. There is no denying, however, that leadership styles are very different, and the results of these styles are very different, too.

Regardless of where you find yourself to be among these five styles, you can, if you really want to, develop democratic leadership behaviors and attitudes. Try it, and ask for feedback from some of your friends who will be candid with you so you can discover how you're coming across—as others see you.

4

Understanding One Another

Every leader wants to be understood. Every member wants to be understood too! Since everyone has this common desire, why is there so much misunderstanding between people? The answer must include an analysis of the three processes that go on continuously in groups—the process of speaking, the process of listening, and the interaction between the two people involved.

Effective communication is the goal. It is achieved when the listener fully understands the speaker, and, furthermore, when there is no doubt in the mind of either person that the message is fully understood. The following are some of the conditions that can get in the way of effective communication.

1. Preoccupation of the listener who is so concerned with the stimuli within himself or herself that the speaker's message is missed entirely.

Speaker: "We cannot afford to miss this great opportunity to sell our downtown clubhouse and relocate in the country, etc., etc., etc."

Preoccupied listener: "Mmmmm, I wonder if my car will be repaired in time for my trip this weekend, mmmmm."

2. Emotional barriers to certain words which cause the listener to recall something in his or her background or present circumstances that interfere with the will to understand the communication.

Speaker: "People who cheat on their income tax returns are criminals in every sense of the word. Here are the reasons I say this . . . bla, bla, bla."

Reactionary listener: "Ooooo, he doesn't know what he's talking about . . . besides, everyone cheats a little, ooooo."

3. *Hostility* between speakers and listeners causing distortion of the message, an attitude of confrontation and fuel for further hostility.

Speaker 1: "Dogs need affection and freedom like everyone else."

Speaker 2: "Dogs should be disciplined and kept on a leash. *People* need affection and freedom!"

Speaker 1: "Well, I'd rather have a dog as a friend than some of the people I know!"

Speaker 2: "Some of the people I know have dog friends because they don't know how to relate to people!"

Speaker 1: "Well, let me tell *you* something Mr. Dog-hater, etc., etc., etc."

(Notice that there are no listeners in the above scenario.)

4. *Concerns about (or differences in) status, prestige, or power* between speaker and listener that cause intimidation, fear, and anxiety. The real message becomes clouded, unclear, and sometimes lost.

Speaker: "As commanding officer of this ship, I want all you deck hands to feel free to make suggestions about your conditions on board at any time. This is a friendly ship. I will not permit it to be any other way."

Subordinate listener: "Wow! I wouldn't dare talk to *HIM* about anything!"

5. *Personal needs* cause the listener to distort messages or not to understand them at all.

Speaker: "Charlie, I like you, but *dating* you is something

else. Besides, I have a headache tonight and sometimes my headaches last a long, long time."
Needful listener: "Wow, I've got a date just as soon as she
feels better!"
6. *The environment* may not be conducive to effective communication.
Speaker: "I'd like to make this point perfectly clear (rumble-
crash-bang-zoom) and, furthermore, now is the
time to (rattle-splash-boom-whirr)."
Environmentally assaulted listener: "Huh?"

The Process of Speaking or Transmitting

Some people find it difficult to say what they mean. Their
ideas are not clearly formed in their mind; they don't know the
correct words to use in conveying the message; their feelings
about themselves and their audience get in the way of clear thinking; they fail to adapt their message to the audience.

"Uh . . . you know what I mean." (I can't say it, but if it's
clear to me, it *must* be clear to you!)

"Uh . . . I haven't thought this out yet, but . . . " (Maybe if I
try to explain it to you, it will all become clear.)

"Uh . . . I just can't communicate with them." (*They* don't
respect or appreciate me . . . , or I never did like people from
there.)

"According to the latest research, bla, bla, bla." (If you don't
understand research jargon, that's your problem!)

It helps to think something through before you speak about
it. Some find it helpful to jot down key points and supporting
evidence, then to organize it all logically before speaking. Others
try out ideas on a helpful friend before expressing them to a
group or to their supervisor. Still others do better in small groups
where the atmosphere is less threatening and where they can become acquainted with the others in the group before getting involved in a weighty discussion.

Whatever the transmitter chooses to do to be effective, the following suggestions may be helpful:

1. *Know your listener(s)*. What is their educational and cultural background? What do they already know or what have they experienced?

2. *Watch your listener(s) for clues*. Are they listening? Do they understand you? Watch for their frowns or smiles, their head shaking or nodding.

3. *Know your key point(s) before you start talking*.

4. *Make your important point(s) with an example* or by saying them several different ways.

5. *Be as concise as possible* yet thorough enough to be clear.

6. *Enlarge your vocabulary to meet the occasion*. Jot down words others are using that are new to you and check these out in a dictionary or thesaurus. Then try using them yourself before you forget them.

The Process of Listening

Listening is more than the physical process of hearing. Hearing is done simply with our ears. Listening, however, is much more complex. It is both a thinking and an emotional process. Its goal is to achieve meaning and understanding.

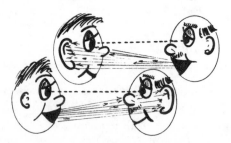

Remember, the listener has this advantage: the normal rate of speech is about 100 to 150 words per minute; whereas, the average rate of thought is about 400 to 450 words per minute. Use this differential to reflect upon content and to search for meaning.

Here are some suggestions to help the listener who wants to become more effective in communicating:

1. Give yourself a reason or purpose for listening. For example: "I'll be better informed; the speaker will respect me; I'll be able to ask better questions; I may get that job offer or promotion; I may earn better grades."

2. *Suspend initial judgment* while listening. Keep your emotions and intellect totally involved in trying to understand.

3. *Resist distractions* such as noises, views, people. Focus totally on the speaker.

4. *Delay responding* until the speaker is finished. Responding too soon will detract from your overall analysis of what is being said.

5. *Repeat verbatim* the key points of the speaker's message when it is important to remember them, or

6. *Rephrase* the key points in your own words if that will help you remember them.

7. *Catch the important theme* of the message. "Listen through" less relevant material for the central points and supporting statements.

8. *Summarize* when you have absorbed all the material you can hold. Interrupt the speaker to do this (if necessary and when possible and appropriate).

The Process of Interaction

"Perfect" communication is seldom attained without verbal interaction between the parties who are speaking and listening. This is true whether there are only two people involved or when a speaker is addressing a large audience.

Furthermore, verbal interaction is not the whole story of effective communication. Some authorities on communication attest that *up to 93 percent of interpersonal communication is non-verbal.* A whole "vocabulary" of meanings is expressed by countless variations of vocal inflection, facial expression, and "body language."

Those who seek to master the universe of human communication would do well to study the intricacies of the voice, the eyebrow, the forehead, and the mouth, not to mention the shoulders, head, and hands—the whole body.

In a typical communication situation between two people, helpful non-verbal behavior includes:

Eye contact that is attentive and searching.

Body posture that projects being interested.

Facial expressions that express the degree of understanding such as smiling, nodding, head shaking, frowning, and raising eyebrows.

Realizing how important non-verbal communication is and accepting the unlikelihood that two people can really reduce their communication effort to words alone, we are primarily concerned with methods of improving our verbal interaction in this chapter.

The whole notion of a person having the right to ask questions in order to understand a speaker is part of what democracy is all about. The right to answer questions in one form or another is a fundamental difference between autocratic behavior and democratic behavior. People have a right to know what is being said and to understand its meaning.

● When the speaker has failed to deliver the message clearly, ask a question to clarify the situation.

"Would you please say (explain) that again? It wasn't clear to me."

● When the speaker has given incomplete information, phrase a question to get more information:

"I understand the three points you have made, Dr. Watson, but aren't there some other things known about this subject that would help us make the right decision?"

"You have given several good reasons for endorsing your project, Mrs. Adams, would you be willing to tell us the arguments of the opposition?"

● When you think you understand the speaker and you want to be sure about it, try putting the message in your own words for the speaker's agreement.

"Kathy, did I understand you to say that we can go ahead on the project as long as we have written approval from the executive committee and as long as we don't exceed $200?"

● When exact wording is required, as in stating a motion in parliamentary procedure, you should repeat exactly what was said and ask for the speaker's agreement.

"It has been moved by Mr. West that 'we purchase up to 20 tickets at $4.50 each for the benefit concert and that every guest must be accompanied by a club member'; is that correct Mr. West?"

● Perhaps the most difficult question of all is the one that challenges the authenticity of the speaker's statement.

"Mrs. Collins, I believe you stated that there are more uncontrolled dogs in our neighborhood than anywhere else. Could you be a little more explicit? That is, do you know what the facts are and where they came from?"

Interpersonal communication is an essential skill for everyone involved in group membership and group activities. Although every member should be aware of the "art of interpersonal communication," it is the presiding officer who must take the initiative to help people understand one another.

This can be done by setting a good example yourself, both as a speaker who is concerned about being heard and understood and as a listener who wants to hear and understand others. It can also be attained by encouraging and complimenting others when they show effective communication behavior. You can become more skilled in communication by learning effective behavior and then practicing it with others who are willing to exchange feedback with you. You may even find it important enough to bring another person into the practice session as an observer to offer helpful suggestions.

You will be well on your way to becoming an effective leader when you add this skill to your personal style and use it consistently.

Part

2

The Techniques

Now, nobody's perfect, and no one is perfectly competent in handling each one of the many group leadership situations that will arise during the course of a year or so; but, once the group leader acquires a **knowledge** *of the various techniques and processes available,* **practice** *is the road that leads to totally effective leadership.*

Three general competencies are required of the totally effective leader.

> *1. You must have a complete repertoire of group techniques or processes. That is, you should have the* **know-how** *to guide the members of a group in a variety of ways. You must be able to help them express their ideas and feelings, to become acquainted with one another, to open up their individual motivational systems, and to solve problems together. And you must make presentations clear and meetings interesting.*
>
> *2. You must have a sense of awareness and sensitivity about group dynamics so that you'll know just when a particular technique or process will do what needs to be done.*
>
> *3. You must have the necessary* **flexibility** *and* **confidence** *in your own leadership style to be able to "shift gears" easily from one technique or process to another.*

Each of these general competencies takes both knowledge and practice. Part 2 focuses upon eight specific techniques or processes and provides you with the information from which to start. Practice, though, is the key to being able to use them well. It will help you develop a feeling for when to use each one, as well as give you the flexibility and confidence you'll need to add a new kind of vitality to your organization.

5

Personal Agenda

In the life of any group there are occasions when the members get together for the first time. Perhaps they have been just appointed or elected to the group; a group may have been formed just to discuss a neighborhood problem; maybe it's the first meeting of the year after a long recess; or maybe it's the first session of a convention, conference, or workshop. There are also times when a group has internal problems or conflicts that call for everyone involved to get together and work things out. Whatever the situation, there are several people present—5, 10, or 50 or more—and chances are pretty good that they will all have something on their minds.

The traditional way of getting things started is to have someone who is designated as the leader, or perhaps a planning committee, present an agenda of problems or issues that should be discussed. The next step is usually to hand out a check list, form buzz groups, or try some brainstorming to get people involved. Or perhaps it's been decided to use an informal discussion, a panel symposium or forum, or one or more of those other tactics described in Part 3 to get things started. These are *all* time-proven methods, and each has its place in helping people become better informed or meaningfully involved.

The *personal agenda* is still another method. It's a way of turning the agenda over to the members immediately, with no screening committee or designated organizer. The personal agenda session is based upon the premise that every person present has something on his or her mind that is related to the reason for the meeting. It also assumes that each of them would like the opportunity to say something to somebody, or to everybody.

The personal agenda is designed to provide for this need, to get things off members' minds or out in the open, and to do it early in the session. It is also designed to offer individuals a choice of follow-up groups with common interests to sharpen their ideas on one another in whatever endeavor it is they wish to pursue.

The process is simple, and it really works. After everyone is welcomed and the circumstances that led to the meeting are briefly described, each person is asked to jot down some key points on a piece of paper, those which are uppermost on his or her mind and which have a direct bearing on the issue. Individuals are asked to follow one of the formats below:

1. *an idea* or thought or belief
2. *a statement* of fact or opinion
3. *a question* or need for facts
4. *a problem* that should be solved

Give them two or three minutes of silence to do this individually, then ask them, one at a time to express their *idea, statement, question,* or *problem.* Appoint a timekeeper, or do it yourself, and limit each person's time to not more than three minutes. You will find that some people and some groups take more time than others. For example, teenagers generally express themselves in a very few sentences. Older people take longer, and professional people take the longest of all—especially philosophers and educators. In any event, select a definite time limit for each person, and designate a timekeeper to announce when each person's time has expired.

There are **two basic rules.** First, *the time limit is absolute.* When a person's time has expired, there is no extra time available—except perhaps to finish a sentence. This restriction is important in order to manage the overly talkative members and to make sure you hear from everyone in a reasonably short time. Without a time limit this personal agenda process can easily go on and on and on. Second, the person speaking has an absolute license to speak for three minutes. *No one is permitted to interrupt* for any reason, and everyone is encouraged to listen attentively.

When each one has presented his or her idea, statement, question, or problem, interaction between and among members is encouraged. Of course, if the group is quite large (that is, more than about 10 or 15 people), it would be better to form buzz groups (Chapter 9) and coordinate their results. For some situations and with large groups, it is best to select a few of the key issues expressed and then ask individuals to get together in small groups, each with a different topic. Let's consider a couple of examples of how the personal agenda session really works.

During the First Meeting

All 10 selected members have arrived. A few seem to know each other, some are introducing themselves, others stand nervously alone waiting for things to start. They have all been invited by the chairperson of the County Planning Commission to discuss the feasibility of developing a small lake area into a county park.

"Good evening everybody, let's all find a chair and move into a small circle so we can see and hear each other. . . . My name is Barny Bostrom, Chairperson of your County Planning Commission, and I'm glad you could all come tonight." (After some sort of get-acquainted activity [Chapter 6], he continues.) "We're here to study the feasibility of developing Laguna Lake into a county park, and each of you has been recommended by a member of the Board of Supervisors as being interested in recreational development or in having experience with some aspect of this project."

"In order to get each of you right into the discussion, we're going to structure this first part of the meeting a little. Will each of you please think about the development of Laguna Lake into a county park and jot down your present thoughts on it. Please come up with one of the following: an idea; a statement; a question; or a problem. Do this during the next minute or two, do it individually, and write whatever notes you want. I've put these four things on the newsprint pad up here so you can all see them."

After all have finished . . . "O.K., now, starting with Jerry, please take up to two minutes to present your choice of these four things to the group. No one is to talk except Jerry and when she is finished, we will move right on to Steve and then Ron, etc., until everyone has spoken. After everyone has spoken, we'll have time to discuss openly whatever we choose. O.K., Jerry, it's yours for two minutes."

Jerry speaks, "I have a *question*. I want to know who owns the property around the lake. I've been told that the county owns the north half and that several individuals own the other half. Can we develop the county side alone without consulting the other owners? And what about our liability for damage done to adjoining property by people using the park? We need to consider all these things before we do anything else."

Steve follows, "I have a *statement* based on my experience with a similar water project in Plumas County. . . ."

And so it goes until each has finished. If you have had someone writing the key points of each speaker on a newsprint pad, you'll have a ready summary to use as a guide for the follow-up discussion. For fairly complex issues like that presented in this example, it may be advisable to "go around the circle" two or more times to be sure that all the ideas, statements, questions, and problems are out in the open early. Although structured, it does get everyone involved, and the best thoughts of the group can then be refined through more informal discussion.

To Reduce Internal Conflict

Nine people work in an office and share the facilities of a little kitchen complete with refrigerator, coffee-maker, sink, and storage closet for cups, dishes, and supplies. The supervisor, who works in another area, has designated Catherine as the manager of the kitchen, with explicit instructions that it shall always be absolutely clean. He adds, "It's your responsibility from now on, Catherine, so please don't bother me with details." Catherine takes her assignment seriously, but some of the other employees are not as neat and tidy as they could be. They leave unwashed cups and dishes and spilled food and beverages around the area without cleaning it up. Catherine loses her patience and posts a system of fines for infractions of the rules. Then she posts on the refrigerator notices to individuals, announcing the number of times they have been fined and how much they owe. Notes on the refrigerator to one another get more and more personal until the atmosphere is just slightly less than open warfare. The situation comes to the attention of the supervisor who decides to call a meeting.

"Good morning, everybody. Let's all find chairs and move into a small circle so we can see and hear each other. . . . I'm aware that we have a little problem in keeping the kitchen neat and clean, and I think we should talk about it. You're all 'top flight' workers, and the teamwork in the office has been excellent. It's too bad that a little thing like how to keep the kitchen clean has tarnished some good friendships.

"I'd like each of you to think quietly for about two minutes. Think about how we can keep that little kitchen clean with the least amount of hassle. Please jot down your *ideas, questions, statements,* or *problems* individually, and then we'll take turns expressing how to best handle this situation."

The rest of the personal agenda process is obvious. Everyone has a part in resolving the issue, and it is very likely that a consensus solution will be reached which everyone will support.

In summary, the personal agenda process, without much initial preparation, is an excellent way to open up discussion among a group of strangers or people in conflict. The agenda comes right out of the group in the form of various ideas, statements, questions, and problems. There is no way anyone can avoid being involved, and when it's all over, people will generally be supportive of the final outcome. Remember to warn group members that this process starts out by being fairly structured, so they will not become upset later when they are told to listen to several speakers consecutively without speaking themselves. And remember to keep the process on a relatively strict timetable. Once you've tried this process a few times, you'll learn just when to use it and when to make little variations in it from time to time to give your membership a change of pace.

6

Getting People Acquainted

Before people will discuss or work together on a common problem effectively, they must know each other. Furthermore, they must be relaxed and at ease. Have you ever noticed a group of people just before a meeting? As they wait for it to begin, there is a buzz of conversation. Everybody is talking to everybody else. They're gathered in groups discussing the weather, Mrs. Smith's new dress, income taxes, the local basketball team's chances of winning the league championship, all sorts of things. Then someone indicates that the meeting is about to start. The groups break up. They take their seats. And now what happens? Dead silence. Everybody is waiting for someone to break the ice.

Even in a small group this is likely to happen, and the larger the group, and the less well acquainted everyone is with everyone else, the deeper and more profound the silence.

As a leader of any small discussion group, your first job is to help each person relax and to get members acquainted with each other so that they'll be in the mood to talk. There are a number of ways to do this, but regardless of which one you use, there are two good general rules to follow:

1. *Introduce yourself first, and do it in the way in which you wish them to introduce themselves.* People in groups want a leader to follow, and they want a pattern set for them. It's your job to set the pattern. If you would like to know not only the names of the members but also their connection with and their interest in the problem under discussion, give your name and describe briefly your contacts and interests, and then ask them to do the same.

2. *Let them hear their own voices just as soon as possible, speaking on a topic they can address easily and well.*

Among the tried and effective ways of getting people acquainted with each other in discussion-sized groups are the following:

Introduce the participants yourself. If you know them all, and the group is small, this is the quickest (and probably the most used) but certainly the least effective way. It won't allow them to talk nor put them at ease. Neither can you possibly introduce any member of even a small group as well as each could do it personally. You generally know very little about each person to begin with, and you're not as interested in that person as he or she is in himself or herself.

Ask each one to make a self-introduction. After you break the ice by introducing yourself and telling a little about yourself in terms of your interest in the subject of the meeting, ask one person at a time to stand, give his or her name, and do the same. This works well for a small group. Stress first names and nicknames. No one can be bothered in a really good discussion with the more formal modes of address. When you introduce yourself, say, "I'm Sadie Smith," not "I'm Mrs. Franklyn Smith," and ask that the members do the same.

So, with a small group, a good lead-in might sound something like this:

> The first thing we want to do here this evening is to get acquainted or *better* acquainted with each other. Let's introduce ourselves. I'll start it off, and after I've introduced me, you introduce you. And tonight, let's forget being Mister, Miss, Ms., or Mrs. Introduce yourself by the name you like to be called or by the name your friends call you—either your first name or your nickname, or both, because that's the way we're going to address you during this meeting. I'm Betty Brown. My interest in discussing this school lunch program lies in the fact that I have three school-age children who eat lunch at school at least once a week. Now, starting over here, will each of you give us your name—first name, please—and tell us briefly about your special interest in this topic.

This will get your meetings off to a good start, since you will be accomplishing these things:

1. You'll know, if you listen, the names of your group members and you'll get a clue as to their attitudes toward the problem or topic.

2. You'll be able to get everyone to say something within the first few moments of the meeting.

3. You'll put everyone at ease because everyone will have actually *said* something, and the next time it will be easier for him or her to do so because the ice has been broken.

4. You'll make it easy for each member to identify with the group and to feel secure in the setting because you will have asked everyone to talk about something that is familiar.

5. You'll set the stage for the informality that encourages free discussion by stressing the use of first names rather than formal titles. This is a good method and a widely used one, but so widely used that sometimes it is well to vary it so:

Have each one make a self-introduction, and then see how well each person can remember the names of the others. Try it this way. Start out just as though you were going to have each one introduce himself or herself. Let the first five or six introduce themselves and tell their stories. When you get to about the seventh, ask not only for a self-introduction but for reintroductions of the five or six preceding people. If anyone can't do it, let the rest of the group help out. (A note of caution. If No. 7 is obviously a shy, retiring individual, go on to the next. You'll be hated if you don't.) Then continue individual introductions for three or four more and then ask another person to introduce *all* of those preceding him or her. Continue this until the last person in the ring has the job of introducing the entire group. This technique will go a long way towards getting people acquainted and breaking the ice.

Another variation, and one which works well with small groups, is to:

Have each one introduce his or her neighbor. This will work whether the group is seated around a table, in a circle, or in rows. Simply announce that you will ask people to introduce whoever's on their left, and give them a moment or two to introduce themselves and to get the information they need for the introduction. It's wise to specify the kind of information you're after in order to keep them under control. Then pick a starting place, either at the end of the row or at some break in the circle, and select the person to start the introductions. Before long each one will be trying to outdo the other in presenting his or her "new friend" to the group.

Still another variation, and one that works especially well in cases where many in the group are total strangers to each other, is to:

Use name plates. This works so well that it should be standard operating procedure whenever the conference group is seated around a table or tables.

In this method, you begin with having everyone introduce himself or herself; you still stress first names and nicknames, but you have each person write out his or her own name plate and leave it in plain sight where everyone can refer to it during the meeting.

All this takes is a supply of marking pens and enough 5- x 8-inch cards for all members. As you open the meeting, state again that you want them to get acquainted, and that since it's easy to forget names, you want them to make their own name plates. Fold your own card in the middle so that it forms a tent with each side 2½ x 8 inches. Then print your first name in large capital letters and your last name in smaller capital letters below it, and set it on the table in front of you so that all can see it. Better yet, print your name on both sides. All that's left to do is for the rest of the members to make out their name plates and set them on the table.

When they have all finished, introduce yourself verbally as in the preceding methods, and have each member of the group do the same.

With this device, not only do first names immediately become the standard mode of address but also the cards will be referred to time and again by members and by yourself when names are forgotten. (Caution. Don't destroy these cards if you're going to be meeting again with these same people. They'll ask for them at the second meeting, and you'll be embarrassed if you don't have them.)

Here are five ways, then, of getting acquainted. Use them, and experience will teach you other perhaps more effective methods or variations of these which you can use to break the ice, to put people at ease, and to make them feel good about speaking out on the issues. Just remember, the sooner you can get people to talk, the better. And the method that opens up the greatest number of people the most quickly is your best. (Note: Different kinds of groups require different kinds of openers. Experiment, and learn to judge what's best for when.)

For other successful methods of getting people acquainted, see *Leadership Is Everybody's Business.*[1]

---

[1]John D. Lawson, Leslie J. Griffin, Randy D. Donant, *Leadership Is Everybody's Business,* Impact Publishers, Inc., San Luis Obispo, California, 1976.

7

Group Motivation

The highest praise that can be given to any meeting is "That was *really* interesting!" The most damning criticism—"What a drag!" Interest is the fountain of attention and action. It is what starts us to thinking and keeps us alert. We think only about the things which interest us. We are "turned off" to thinking about ideas, projects, and topics that don't. Interest is the catalyst of group action. Interest is like a fire. It's much easier to get started and to keep going than it is to rekindle after it has gone out. The key, then, is to *get* your group members interested, and then *keep* them that way.

How can you make your meetings interesting? How can you get and keep members of a group interested? The person who puts into action the answers to these questions will be making a tremendous stride toward becoming an effective group leader.

Interested people are motivated people. But access to an individual's motivational system is complex indeed. If we knew the answer to this mystery of human behavior, we could open the gates of productivity and creativeness beyond all dreams.

Since we are associated with stable people, that is, people who are not overly troubled by the fear of death, the threat of physical injury, or the possibility of losing their life's savings or their jobs, we can identify three basic states of motivation.

Awareness—"I am aware of a particular element (or group of elements) in the environment that meets my needs or hopes. Without it (them) I feel incomplete, unsatisfied."

Anticipation—"I believe this goal is attainable; I think I can do it."

Emotion—"I'll turn on my energy valve a little (or a lot) and get it (or do it)."

● *Awareness and interest are interrelated.* A person who is really interested in birds or automobiles or food will give attention to these things over all others—browsing in a bookstore, walking along the road, or planning a vacation. One is more *aware* of things of personal interest than of anything else in the environment. In an organization, not everyone will be equally interested in or aware of any single program or project. This is a fundamental truth about people that the leader must understand, accept, and adjust to. There is no way an individual can be motivated by another person to become a bird-lover, an automobile-enthusiast, or a food-fanatic if that person does not feel that personal sense of fulfillment or satisfaction will result from his or her doing so.

● *The anticipation of achievement,* the hope of attaining a goal and the confidence that success will come from trying are essential to motivation too. "If I join this club *I will* meet people and develop friendships." "If I am elected president, *I can* develop a sense of teamwork and contribute to the quality of life in my neighborhood." People may be both aware of and interested in taking part in the activities of an organization, but they may not become fully involved because of a low self-concept and the fear of failure. These individuals can overcome this cause of apathy if they are given encouragement and the opportunity to experience small successes; playing a small part on a large team is a start, and giving them some training in certain skills will help too.

● *Emotion* is the valve that turns on personal energy. People are around and literally "turn themselves on" when they are *aware* of an environmental factor which relates to their personal needs or hopes and when they believe they can achieve the goals of having these needs and hopes met. "Turning on" and "turning off" is something people do to themselves. It is *a change in energy level.* The initial amount of energy the individual exerts depends on: (1) the values—the strength of the beliefs in focus and (2) the expected outcome—the consequences of involvement.

One of the tragedies of poor leadership occurs when the elected leader gets "turned on" to a particular goal and gets so strongly motivated to get something done that he or she fails to take the time to involve the membership in the necessary discussions designed to raise the level of the group members' awareness of their own needs that can be met by turning *themselves* on and getting involved.

In the following paragraphs nine procedures to use in making meetings more interesting are described. An explanation of *why* these procedures arouse interest is also given. Notice how many are based on the natural impulses that all people possess.

Techniques to Get and Keep Interest

1. Encourage and sustain participation. Everyone wants to get involved to some degree or he or she wouldn't be there. So get your group members into the act as soon as possible. Keep your introductory remarks short—eliminate them entirely if you can. Use project checklists to let them identify the problems they wish to discuss. Let them feel that they are taking important roles, that the meeting is theirs. People like to be doing something—to obey that activity impulse. Let them.

2. Show your own interest. A "dead pan" may be an asset in a poker game or in a business deal, but not in a chairperson or group leader. When members of the group speak, give them your undivided attention. Look at them and listen to them. Don't gaze out of the window or doodle notes. Your actions speak louder than your words. Don't *tell* them how interested you are. *Show* it. Interest is infectious. It spreads. If you indicate by your manner that the subject really is vital to you and that you feel it is equally vital to them, they'll gradually take the same attitude. As soon as a few of the leaders in the group (initiator, orientator, facilitator, etc.)

catch the spirit, it will infect the others.

This works in reverse too, by the way, so if you're bored or indifferent, or act that way, you can expect the same reaction from other members of the group.

3. Identify and call on the interested members first. Just as the leader's initial interest in the subject will infect others, so will the contagion spread from member to member. As you start your meeting, then, watch for those who seem to have caught the spark, and direct questions to them. As others begin to wake up, you can bring them into the discussion. Don't call on the quiet one over in the far corner until you have the others involved and the quiet one has had time to warm up a little.

4. Use humor. This doesn't mean that you have to be a TV comic. It doesn't even mean that you have to be able to tell a funny story. As a matter of fact, if you're the kind of person who just can't tell a story and make it really funny (and most of us are), avoid it entirely. There's nothing unfunnier than an *allegedly* funny story.

You will truly find some clever people, though, in almost any group. Laughing at wisecracks will encourage others to do the same. Often some catch phrase or a slip of the tongue can bring out the grins and the chuckles better than a planned gag or story. In a meeting recently, a member solemnly declared, "We should leave no stern untoned to get this job done!" The group had a great time "untoning sterns" for the remainder of that meeting, and got the job done efficiently as well.

Nothing seems to draw a group together more quickly or develop a "we" spirit of easiness more naturally than a good laugh. Develop the ability to go along with whatever gag crops us. Smile and laugh with the membership and give them a chance to smile and laugh with you.

5. Make everyone feel important. Everyone likes approval; most everyone likes the spotlight; all like a sense of accomplishment. Take advantage of this. Show approval when someone makes a contribution that is worthwhile, and be complimentary of the person who has anything to say—especially any of the non-leader types.

Recently, a folk dancing instructor had a group of beginners "do-si-do-ing" in the multi-purpose room of the local school. As they rather awkwardly finished a set, she turned off the record player and told them, "You're wonderful! You really did that beautifully!" And did they feel good! Do we love approbation? We eat it up! So be an encourager and satisfy that need that we all have for a pat on the back.

Give everyone a chance to be in the spotlight. When you know someone who has had a relevant experience in a specific area, say, "Fred, you're pretty close to this problem and know more about it than the rest of us, what do you think about it?" Give Fred and Sue and all the rest their turn to shine, and watch them expand and their interest grow. Remember, the parties that were the most fun and which stick in your memory were the ones where *you* were the center of attention. The ones that bored you were the ones where you were ignored. It's just the same in a meeting.

When the group has thought through a problem well and has come up with a good solution, call attention to it. As you summarize, highlight the fact that progress is being made and that something is being accomplished. Nothing is more frustrating than lack of progress—so when you do get progress, call attention to it.

These three—*love of approval, love of prominence,* and *love of progress*—are strong components of interest. Be on the lookout for ways to use them. Often when you *could* operate alone as a leader, it is a good practice to designate and use a recorder, a consultant, and an observer. This will be more effective and worthwhile since you'll be sharing the stage with three others and at the same time giving them prominence.

6. *Arouse their curiosity.* There's hardly a stronger impulse in most of us than curiosity. Notice the reaction in any meeting when a latecomer opens the door. Everyone turns in unison to see who it is. A fire siren brings everyone to the window or outside to see where the fire engines are headed. How can you use this?

When you ask a question, never (or rarely) designate the person to answer before you state the question. Instead, ask the question of no one in particular—pause, look around the room, and observe anxiety/anticipation levels rise as they wait for you to announce the name of the person to respond. This is valuable for other purposes, too. It promotes thinking by everyone; it builds up suspense (another good interest factor), and it provides a change of pace.

Run the numbers ahead when recording on a chart or chalkboard. Suppose at a PTA meeting the discussion centers around "What can we do to improve our schools?" The leader has put the question to the group, and one suggestion has been forthcoming. The chalkboard or chart might look like this:

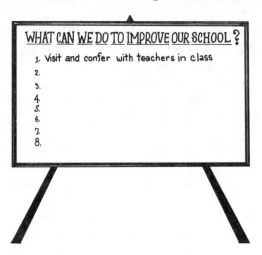

The seven blanks encourage the members to think, "Well, there must be at least seven more. I wonder what they are?"

Use a "strip tease" when displaying and talking from charts. Cover the message on the chart or graph with strips of paper fastened at the ends with thumb tacks or scotch tape. Pull off the strips to uncover each part as you discuss it, so that the group sees only what you *have* talked about and *are* talking about, and is left to wonder what you're going to uncover next. Closely allied in some ways to curiosity, *suspense* is another strong interest factor. This is what keeps some of us up until three in the morning reading detective stories. (We just can't stop until we find out who killed the butler.)

7. *Present all sides.* In formal business meetings, it is the duty of the presiding officer to see to it that following a speaker *favoring* the motion under consideration there should be a speaker *opposing* it. This, of course, is primarily to make sure that both sides have a fair hearing. However, this practice has another outcome. Recognizing and giving the floor first to the proponents and then to the opponents of a proposal keeps the issue in doubt—doubt builds suspense, and suspense builds interest. Similarly in an informal discussion, try to identify those who favor various sides of the problem under consideration. Then bring them into the discussion in rotation so that both or all sides are kept from piling up a preponderance of favorable evidence. Help the proponents of the less popular side by making suggestions and asking leading questions, but keep from showing which side *you* favor. As long as you can maintain a reasonable balance in the arguments pro and con, you will sustain interest and suspense. As soon as the issue is decided, the interest dies.

8. *Keep your meeting free from distracting influences.* It's pretty difficult to keep your attention on two things at once. Uncomfortable chairs, too much or too little heat, noises from outside the meeting room—all serve to distract attention from the subject at hand. Get to your meeting place ahead of time, and see that it is as free as possible from these upsetting influences.

Many leaders lay themselves wide open to another type of divided attention by passing out copies of printed, mimeographed, or other kinds of reading matter, and then trying to continue a discussion. *Don't ever do this!* If the material is important enough to merit such action, stop the discussion right then and let everyone read it. If it doesn't need to be read immediately, distribute it after the discussion. Nothing can be more futile (or more dissonant) than to ask people to listen, discuss, and read at the same time. You'll probably *lose* their interest in the process.

How you dress can be a distracting influence, too. In your desire to make a good appearance, don't dress up! Wear something appropriate but comfortable, something that puts you at ease. You don't want to focus the attention of the group on you more than is really necessary. A too-bright pair of socks, an obviously new suit, or a low-cut dress can distract attention just about as much as a fire siren. Perhaps more, for the siren stops eventually, but those red socks with the purple and green stripes stay as long as you do.

9. *Keep things moving.* The leader of a discussion meeting has to play it by ear; perhaps it is more fitting to say that the leader has to conduct by ear. This requires sensing when things begin to drag, then speeding up the tempo; getting the feel of correct timing and seeing that it is maintained. No amount of pre-planning will accomplish this. It will help, but often the group will refuse to follow the script you have so carefully prepared. Some monopolizer will get carried away and will seem to have no sense of terminating whatever. The wanderer may have been day-dreaming just when the issue was being decided, and you may have to explain it again especially for him. You may have to get up-front and interrupt your motor-mouthed member. Whatever you can do to keep things moving and to keep time from being wasted is worth doing. *People like to see their meetings move; they like to get somewhere.* They lose interest quickly if things drag.

One specific thing you can do to keep things moving is watch your own timing. When you have a comment to make, make it brief. Don't fall into the habit of repeating and rewording contributions made by members. If they don't say it exactly the way you would, ask them if they mean thus and so, or accept it as stated. Don't try to put your words into their mouths.

10. *Change the pace.* Almost as bad as too slow a pace is to maintain the same tempo and the same routine all the time. Again you'll have to play it by ear to sense when a change is needed. If the group has been debating an issue for some time and getting nowhere, break in and summarize the discussion, bringing out the points which have been made for and against the proposal, or call on your observer to analyze and sum up. Vary your procedure in presenting problems. Introduce role playing (Chapter 9) where it can be done.

Don't always use a chalkboard to record progress; try newsprint or simply have the recorder keep the notes at his or her seat.

Break up into buzz groups (Chapter 9) when the problem gets too complicated for the group to solve as a whole. The interest span of an adult group is longer than of one composed of children or teen-agers, but it, too, has a breaking point. Do what you can to see that this point is never reached.

If you can make your meetings interesting, you'll take a giant step toward making them worthwhile. Since getting and keeping people interested is more of an art than an exact science, practice these techniques until you can do them smoothly, and you'll get good results.

1. Get everybody into the act as soon as you can.
2. Be interested yourself, and show it.
3. Direct questions to interested members first.
4. Don't be afraid of chuckles and laughs; invite humor.
5. Share the spotlight; make everyone feel important.
6. Play on everyone's curiosity.
7. Keep the arguments balanced; maintain suspense.
8. Avoid distracting influences.
9. Watch the tempo.
10. Change the routine.

8

Problem Solving

There are many acceptable methods of introducing a problem to a group for consideration, discussion, and action.

A problem may be:
group leader.
presented by the **group leader.**
presented by a **group member.**
chosen from a **checklist.**

A problem can also be presented in such a way that group members will develop a role-playing exercise to seek its solution. (Role playing is discussed more fully in Chapter 11.) Which method you choose, of course, will be determined by the subject under discussion, the makeup of your group, and the conditions under which you are conducting the meeting. All are good and all have their place.

Group Leader

When it is *your* responsibility to state the problem at hand, state it clearly, definitely, briefly, and as interestingly as possible. Present it as a question, not as a topic or as a statement. And always see that as stated, the question calls for an answer. For a problem is simply a difficulty—a situation which calls for thinking about possible solutions. It may be stated as an actual case which calls for action, or as a general statement of conditions calling for a more general conclusion. A problem which describes an actual situation is generally more interesting and more easily solved than one that deals in generalities. For example, answering the question "How can we overcome the shortage of qualified help?" may be of interest to a group of employers, but stating it as an actual case brings it much closer to home and makes possible a more definite solution.

Group Member

Suppose the group has met to discuss the general problem identified above, *i.e.*, how to respond to the shortage of qualified help. Someone early in the discussion may say, "Well, take my situation. . . ." That's just the opportunity you should be waiting for. Call him or her immediately to the front of the room to describe the problem, and then use the following procedure in conducting the remainder of the discussion.

This particular technique consists of using a chalkboard or newsprint outline to lead the group to the solution by directing it through the seven steps of good thinking. It is a particularly good device, where an actual problem situation exists. The outline looks like this:

Just What Does John (or Sarah) Want to Accomplish?

1. _____
2. _____

Important Facts		Possible Courses of Action
1. _____ 6. _____		1. _____
2. _____ 7. _____		2. _____
3. _____ 8. _____		3. _____
4. _____ 9. _____		4. _____
5. _____ 10. _____		5. _____

Solution

It is best to form a team—a **leader** for the discussion, a **recorder** to write the contributions of the group on the chalkboard or chart, an **observer** to analyze and evaluate progress, and a **consultant** who knows a great deal about the facts involved in the problem.

After these roles are assigned, the leader should:

● *Ask one or more members of the group* to describe the situation clearly and briefly.

● *Help the group to limit and define the problem* by deciding on the most desirable outcome of the situation. Have the recorder put this on the chalkboard or chart. Use questions such as "What is the best thing that could happen in this situation?" and "What do we want to have happen?"

● *Solicit suggestions and opinions* by asking, "Now that you know the situation and what we want to happen, what would *you* do?"

There may be one or two hardy souls who will stick their necks out and volunteer an opinion. If not, use the buzz group and the process described in Chapter 9. Have the recorder list these opinions on the board under "Possible Courses of Action" and write after each solution the initials of the person offering it. If there are *no courses of action* forthcoming, then,

● *Get the important facts.* Ask, "In your opinion, what are the really important facts that should influence our decision?" Have the recorder list them, abbreviating and briefing them as much as possible.

As contributions are made by members of the group, get common agreement that the fact given *is* important.

● *Ask for revisions of courses of action* suggested (if any) and other possible courses of action. Have the recorder list and initial those given.

● *Help the group to weigh facts and decide.* Take the items listed under "Possible Courses of Action" one at a time and ask three questions about each:

1. (To the contributor) "What facts listed support your conclusion? What facts are in conflict?"
2. (To the group) "If we did this, would it accomplish what we want to have happen?"
3. (To the person who described or brought up the problem) "Could you do this?"

If any one alternative fails to measure up to the standards implied by these questions, erase it. And then, after all suggested courses of action have been tested,

● *Ask the group for a conclusion.* Ask for the course of action or combination of courses of action remaining that seems the best. If the members are unable to reach a conclusion as a group, break up into smaller groups for a *buzz session* (Chapter 9). Give them two or three minutes to discuss the possible courses of action and to decide on the best. Then call for reports from each buzz group. It is surprising how much agreement there will be and how quickly a conclusion will be reached.

● *Suggest that the action agreed upon by the group* be implemented and that the results, whether good or bad, be shared with the group at a later date.

With the guidance of an alert leader, this device helps to keep the thinking of the group focused on the problem under consideration. This is a "guided" discussion—almost a "directed" one—but notice that the leader never tells the group *what* to think, but only *how* to think. So, even though the discussion is fairly structured and controlled, it is entirely democratic.

Whether this method with its formalized, rather rigid pattern is used in a discussion or not, it is still an excellent guide for discussions that have the solution of a problem as their goal.

The eight steps listed here mirror the process that a group (as well as an individual) goes through in working out a difficulty. Not only do these steps constitute the thought process that we generally use, but also they are the basic steps of *good thinking*. See that your group follows them.

Problem Checklist

A problem checklist is no more than a listing of common difficulties which the leader feels the group may have encountered and therefore may wish to discuss. The sample checklist entitled "Some Pressing Problems in Wholesale Credit" was prepared to open a meeting of credit managers.

The purpose of such a checklist is to suggest problems to the group members that might be troubling them; from those listed they can choose the one or several they would prefer to discuss.

To use this device, have enough pre-prepared lists duplicated so that each member may have a copy. Distribute them as the meeting opens and ask members to check the ones they have been most aware of recently. When you see that they have finished, read the list aloud, pausing after each problem to find out how many have checked it. Mark the ones receiving the most votes on your copy. When you have gone through the list in this manner, you will find four or five that the group considers most important. Then simply ask which one of these it wishes to discuss first and start the discussion.

This device is one of the best ways of getting the meeting

under way when only the general subject (not the specific problems) has been identified beforehand. Note that it gets all members involved in the group process immediately.

In preparing a problem checklist, pay attention to the example that follows. Notice that the difficulties listed are general in statement and scope. You may not be a credit manager yourself, but the odds are you will find some things you could check, too.

Some Pressing Problems in Wholesale Credit

(Do you ever have to handle any of these?)

1. Under-financed businesses (lacking working capital)

2. Over-expansion of retailers

3. Taxes

4. Inexperienced retailers

5. Shortage of qualified help

6. Scarcities of merchandise

7. High prices

8. Competitive selling—using credit to expand sales

9. Rising cost of inventories

10. Diminishing returns and expanding overhead

11. Pending government controls

12. Inadequate information on financial statements

13. Lack of coordination between credit and sales force

14. Lack of adequate accounting by retailers

15. Poor follow-up on past due accounts

16. Requests to return merchandise

17. Requests for extension of terms

18. Too-free extension of credit

19. Lack of information on credit reports, both new and old accounts

20. No adequate system for keeping credit files current

Leading Group Thinking

Leading a group discussion is really helping people to think through a problem and to arrive at a solution, a conclusion, or a decision. Therefore, it is important that you, as a leader, know *how* people *think.* Let's review how we think as individuals in order to better understand how we may think in groups. The following section illustrates how our mental processes operate when we tackle a problem calling for a decision (a choice between two or more courses of action). We think in much the same way and go through the same steps in the solution of almost any problem.

The Way We Think	An Example
1. We *face* a problem or difficulty.	1. Shall I trade in the old car on a new one or keep it another year or two?
2. We *define, limit,* and *clarify* the problem.	2. My car is eight years old and has gone nearly 100,000 miles. It still runs pretty well, but the motor is noisy, and the body is full of squeaks and rattles. The paint is okay but dingy; the upholstery on the front seat has a hole in it. We'd have to arrange with the bank to pay for a new car on installments, but if we get a good trade-in, I guess we could pay cash.
3. We form an *opinion,* a *tentative conclusion,* a guess as to the probable answer to our problem.	3. I believe I'll trade it in on a new car if I get a decent trade-in allowance on the old one.
4. We find *facts* to back up our opinion or oppose it.	4. I take my car downtown and talk to the dealer. He looks it over and offers me what he calls the "Blue Book" value. It isn't as much as I had expected. He takes me for a ride in a new car. Wow, it's beautiful; it even smells good. I talk to Andy, my neighbor, who just traded his old car in on a new one. He says, "Yeah they're nice, all right, but you'll have to wash, polish, and clean it up every week. With the old crate, I just let it stay dirty." I'm aware that the new one uses lots of gas, too. I stop in at the bank, and they say they'll finance the deal if I decide to buy.

(Continued)

The Way We Think	An Example
5. We weigh the *facts* and *change our opinion* on the basis of the facts.	**5.** I talk it over with my wife. We both want a new car. We're tired of the old one. Most of our neighbors have new cars. Pat says she's ashamed to drive it downtown and afraid to take it on a long freeway trip. On the other hand, they won't give us as much as we'd like for our old one, and payments will put a strain on our budget. The old car would do for another year and maybe we could save enough to reduce the payments next year. We haven't had any trouble with the old car lately. It uses a little oil, but it runs all right. My wife finds an article in the morning paper that says car production may be cut drastically, and new cars may be hard to get next year.
6. We reach a *conclusion* based on all available facts.	**6.** I decide to see the dealer once more and if he'll up the trade-in on my old car by $100, I'll buy a new one.
7. We *act* on our conclusion.	**7.** He increases the trade-in allowance, and I'll pick up the new car today.

Since a group must be led through these steps in thinking through and discussing problems, it is important that the group leader knows them well.

Again, these steps are:

1. Recognize a problem or difficulty.
2. Define, limit, and clarify the problem or situation.
3. Form an opinion or inference as to its solution.
4. Get the facts.
5. Weigh the facts and revise opinions if the facts make such a course necessary.
6. Reach a conclusion or solution based on all available facts.
7. Take the action indicated by the conclusion.

Just so you'll be prepared when it happens, be aware that not all individuals or all groups think rationally *all* of the time. Quite often they will fail to follow these steps or will be guilty of sloppy thinking. Some of the most common errors you can help them avoid are these:

1. Failing to define and clarify the problem.
2. Looking for facts before deciding on a tentative solution.
3. Bogging down at Step 3: Forming an opinion and refusing to search for or recognize the facts that pertain to this opinion—"jumping to conclusions," thus omitting Steps 4, 5, and 6 entirely.
4. Failing as a result of bias or prejudice to weigh the facts objectively or to revise their opinions.
5. Being unable to reach a conclusion even when all the facts are in and have been carefully weighed.
6. Failing to act on their conclusions—to follow through.

In short, your job in leading a group of persons through the solution and discussion of a problem is to see that they follow these proven procedures of good thinking and to help them avoid the common pitfalls of sloppy thinking. To do this:

1. *Present the problem* clearly, briefly, and interestingly.
2. *Ask for opinions,* without supporting reasons. Try to get all possible alternatives out in the open.
3. *Call for reasons* for and against each alternative.
4. *Select the alternative* with the most popular support and the greatest chance to succeed.

9

Buzz Groups

One of the best ways to ensure maximum participation in a large group is by means of the buzz session. You'll appreciate how it got its name the first time you see and hear it in operation. The buzz session takes a very natural impulse and puts it to good use. When you have been at a large dinner, say 15 to 20 people, have you ever attempted to keep a conversation going with everyone taking part? Almost impossible! The natural tendency is for you to talk to the person on your right, the one on your left, and the one or two directly across the table from you. Therefore, instead of a general conversation involving all those present, if left to your own devices, you'll break up into conversational groups of five or six. These are natural *buzz sessions.*

In a formal meeting when a slate of candidates is presented and you are asked to vote, isn't it your natural tendency to turn to the person next to you and talk it over first? You probably wouldn't stand up in a meeting and discuss the candidates with everyone, but you'd have few inhibitions about talking it over with the people nearest you.

It seems that in a group of any size, the sheer intimidation of numbers alone keeps most of us from expressing ourselves freely. Only the most uninhibited seem to be entirely free from this fear of "the group" and have the courage to speak up. The rest of us simply keep our thoughts to ourselves. The point at which a group becomes so large that it manages to keep us mute is difficult to measure. Ordinarily, a group of six or eight doesn't have this effect, and in a group this size we are more likely to speak up. When it grows to 12 or 15, the pressure to keep quiet begins to build, and in extremely large groups only a few will be brave enough to contribute.

The buzz session takes advantage of the fact that even the most reticent of us will talk and discuss topics freely in a group of 5 or 6—a freedom seldom felt in a group of 50 or 60.

Arranging a large assembly into buzz groups is easy. If the meeting is in an auditorium with fixed rows of seats, just have the people in each alternate row turn around to face the people behind them and form groups of not more than five or six. Each group should then get acquainted and elect or decide on: (1) *a leader to guide the discussion* and (2) *someone to take notes and report for the group later.* If the room is arranged with moveable chairs, it's even easier, and the buzz groups can be formed into circles so that there can be total eye contact among all members during discussion.

Have you ever noticed that people who come to meetings together usually sit together, all in the same row? It happens almost all the time. Unless you do something about it as you are forming buzz groups, all of them are likely to end up in the same little circle. If you want to liven up the discussion a little, do something to break up these cliques of friends. They already know each other, and they probably think very much alike; such groups are not likely to be very productive.

To work around this, form circles with people who sit one *behind* the other, that is, by columns instead of rows. These buzz groups will probably consist of strangers with a variety of different values and ideas. The discussions of such groups are always more interesting and productive than those groups made up of families and neighbors.

Another effective way to form buzz groups is to have people "count off" aloud in numbers, starting with the person on the end of the first row, then continuing along each row to the very back row. For example, if there are 50 people and you want groups of 5, ask them to "count off" by 10s so you will end up with 10 groups of 5 each. It would go like this: "one," "two," "three," etc. through "ten"; then start over with "one," "two," "three," etc., row by row, through to ten. When forming buzz group circles, then all the "ones" would form a group, the "twos" would form a group, etc., until you have 10 groups of 5 persons each. If you want groups of eight, simply have them count off by eights. The multiples you choose are both a function of the number in your entire group, and the size of buzz sessions you have in mind.

If you find yourself in a situation with "a few danglers" (when you see the multiple doesn't work out just perfectly) simply choose that number of people *before* you do the numbering and ask them to assist you in some way—observing the groups as they progress or distributing or displaying materials for you. This way, your groups will work as you've planned and no one will feel left out.

How and Where to Use a Buzz Group

Perhaps the most effective place for this device is in a symposium or forum where one (or more) speaker delivers an address which is to be followed by questions or comments from the floor. If it is used in a symposium, time should be taken for a short buzz session following each speaker. Paper and pencils should be provided for each group so that the members may record their questions and be ready when the question period arrives. It's amazing how much audience participation is generated this way and how many more intelligent questions and comments are forthcoming. By using this technique there is seldom any danger of encountering those devastating blank silences after the speaker finishes, when the moderator looks to the audience expectantly and asks, "Now, are there any questions?" Instead of hopefully and fearfully addressing his or her query to the audience as a whole, the leader can start things off easily by pointing to any buzz group and asking, "What is the question *your* group wishes to ask the speaker?"

When buzz groups are not used, audience participation in forums and symposia is quite apt to be limited to the few who: (1) love the limelight (whether they have anything to contribute or not), (2) want to show off their knowledge of the subject by taking issue with the speaker, or (3) feel compelled to ask questions to make the speaker feel that he or she was appreciated. As a result, the caliber of the questions asked is quite likely to be a disappointment.

In contrast, the buzz technique gives all persons a chance to talk it over with four or five of their peers before making a "public" response. Questions that might be asked are evaluated and discussed and the obviously silly or trite ones discarded. As a result, the questions are good and quickly forthcoming (a comforting thought for the moderator!).

Other Specialized Uses

The buzz group can be used very effectively in many group settings. Here are just a few:

● *To generate questions* or problems to be considered by conference sections or committees.

● *To consider committee reports* that have been presented to the general assembly. You are all too familiar with what usually happens when a committee makes its report to the larger assembly.

The secretary of the committee either reads his or her report or distributes mimeographed copies to the assembly. When it is presented, the secretary moves its adoption, someone seconds the motion, and without too much consideration, the assembly adopts it—usually without any discussion at all. This is the time to have it considered in a five-minute buzz session before voting on it. It is surprising how quickly and easily errors, inconsistencies, omissions, etc., will be detected by these smaller groups which would have gone unnoticed if they had been considered in the usual manner.

● *To brainstorm* for ideas (such as the possible solutions to a problem or suggestions for possible goals).

● *To nominate officers* or to *select members* for an important committee. In these instances, each buzz group serves as an "on-the-spot" nominating committee. When a name is suggested, someone from the group can easily check the interest of the person under consideration since he or she is probably right there in the room.

● *To vote on a motion or for candidates* during an election, after the motion has been debated by the most knowledgeable proponent and opponent or after the campaign speeches. Individuals, especially those who are somewhat intimidated by large audiences (most of us!), can then discuss the motion or candidates informally, and can even invite them to their buzz groups to answer questions. When all the buzzing and debating is over, individuals vote in the usual way: by "ayes" and "nays," by standing, by raising a hand, or by ballot.

● *To consider an important or difficult problem* which has arisen in an informal business meeting. Breaking up into small groups for an informal discussion often brings forth sound proposals and immediate action. The correct parliamentary procedure is simple.

As more experience is gained with this relatively new group process, it is probable that even more effective uses will be found. In many situations it is well worth the time whenever discussion in a larger group bogs down.

Member: "I move we discuss this matter informally in small groups."

Member: "I second the motion."

Presiding Officer: "You have heard the motion; is there any discussion? Hearing none we shall vote. All those in favor of discussing this matter informally in small groups, say 'aye,' those opposed, say 'nay.' This motion is passed, and we shall now form groups of five or six."

Now, it's *your* job to help get those groups formed.

10

Brainstorming

Most of us would agree that "A man's judgment is no better than his facts." In the same vein, it might be said that the thinking of an individual or a group can be no better than the number of inferences, tentative solutions, and new ideas that can be developed as *possible* solutions to a given problem. There is no doubt that many individuals and many groups often fail to arrive at a satisfactory solution simply because enough possible alternatives are not brought to light and given the consideration which they deserve.

It has been facetiously said that in any group or any organization, for every "idea person" there are 20 "what's the idea" people. In other words, for every one of us who can think constructively, and who can come up with new ideas, there are many others who think negatively and devote most of their time developing reasons why a particular thing can't be done.

As a result, many organizations are now making use of "brain-storming" to bring to light alternative methods—not only for solving problems but also for developing new ideas.

The essential features of a brainstorming session are few and simple.

1. The number of participants should be large enough so that there are potentially many sources of ideas. Brainstorming groups may be anywhere from 10 to 20 or 25 in number.

2. The participants should be of somewhat equal status so that all will feel free to contribute their ideas. They should also have some familiarity with the problem.

3. Arrangements should be made for one or two recorders to take down ideas on chalkboards or newsprint as fast as they are presented. In smaller groups, a tape recorder may also be used to record discussion.

4. The leader states the problem and also makes clear that certain ground rules are to be rigidly observed. These are:

    a. Every idea presented must be *positive.*

    b. There will be *no comments* allowed regarding any idea presented. (Criticism of ideas presented are absolutely forbidden.)

    c. Everyone is encouraged to speak up and to *express ideas regardless of how fantastic* they may seem.

    d. Participants are encouraged to present ideas as *rapidly* as they come to mind. (The only limit on speed should be to permit the recorders to write down the suggestions as they are made.)

    e. Participants are also encouraged to *"hitch-hike"* ideas, which means to add to or revise ideas suggested by other members of the brainstorming team.

This process is strikingly successful. In a recent session in which the author participated, a group of some 30 participants generated 154 ideas for the solution of a difficult administrative problem. Not all of these ideas were workable, of course, and many of them were ordinary, run-of-the-mill, unimaginative solutions which had been tried with only moderate success. Also included in the list were many fantastic suggestions which were obviously unworkable. Out of the chaff of crackpot and routine suggestions, however, came three or four which showed real promise.

One of the most striking outcomes of brainstorming is the way in which a seemingly fantastic idea stimulates someone else to build upon it and change it slightly so that it actually proves to be of value.

After brainstorming sessions, it is essential to evaluate, condense, and bring together the ideas presented; to discard those which obviously are not workable; and to terminate the period with a listing of those which are worthy of further consideration. Buzz sessions (Chapter 9) are especially effective when you want to make a decision during the same meeting. Or a committee can be formed to consider the idea and present a recommendation at the next meeting.

This technique may be used in the solution of all sorts of problems. The following is an illustration of how a seemingly fantastic idea may develop into a usable one. A recent brainstorming session conducted by the extension service in California was devoted to the problem of utilizing grazing lands where there was an inadequate water supply for the livestock which were competing with the wild animals that normally graze on the area.

> The grazing land under consideration was a forested or semi-forested area containing some trees and large shrubs. It was reported that someone in this group, knowing that during hot weather trees and shrubs give off a great deal of moisture into the air through their leaves, came up with the idea of placing plastic envelopes over the trees. The envelopes were to be fitted with channels which would collect the moisture given off by these plants and conduct it into receptacles at the foot of the tree. Thus, a certain amount of water would be collected for the use of livestock and wild animals. The typical skeptic would probably point out that, while trees certainly do give off water, the amount would hardly be sufficient. Furthermore, the cost of these plastic envelopes, which would have to be manufactured especially for this, would be prohibitive, and if these envelopes cov-

ered the tree for an extended period of time, the tree would undoubtedly die. In fact, any number of reasons could be given why such an idea would be patently absurd. Nonetheless, this suggestion went to the evaluating committee. On the committee were some men with imagination. They tried out this idea on a tree and found to their surprise that in not too long a time they had collected 25 gallons of water. The final result was the origin of at least a possible way of putting hundreds and perhaps thousands of acres of land to use, which until that time had been rendered unusable by virtue of the lack of drinking water.

Other equally fantastic stories have been reported as to the value of brainstorming sessions in developing new ideas. And, it can be seen from this description that brainstorming is little more than creative thinking carried on as a group process. It separates positive from negative thinking and divides the *generation* of ideas from their immediate (and often too hasty) *evaluation*.

Brainstorming sessions should not be too long. The leader should be alert to note when the flow of ideas begins to slow down and to be ready with some plan to start them flowing again. Some leaders set a limit of three minutes, and at the end of that time have the brainstormers take a break, stand up, walk around, and discuss anything *except* the problem. After a few minutes they go back to their session again. It seems more logical, however, to play it by ear, and if at the end of the set time the session is still rolling in high gear, delay the break until it slows down.

Brainstorming Sessions for Larger Groups

The key to handling larger groups in brainstorming sessions is to make use of the "buzz session" technique and to break them up into smaller groups. The optimum number for a group that can operate effectively as a single unit is probably around 12 to 15. When the group is larger than that, use the procedure described below:

1. Divide the participants into groups of five or six persons. Ask each group to be seated in a compact circle and to select a leader and a recorder. Give each recorder a pencil and a packet of 5- x 8-inch cards on which to keep a listing of the ideas generated by the buzz group. Ask each group to select a name for itself such as "Braintrusters," "Aces," "Mental Giants," any name which comes to mind. Record the names on chalkboard or newsprint.

2. *Put the participants through a warm-up session.* A good device to use is a picture or cartoon; ask them to name it or give it a title. Introduce some competition by challenging each group to come up with the largest number of names in three minutes. At the end of that time ask each recorder to count the number of names his or her group had generated. List on the chart the number brainstormed by each group, add the totals, and call attention to the large number of titles developed by the entire group. It is not improbable that each group would have found 15 to 20 titles.

3. *Have a short evaluation session.* This should emphasize the separation of *generating* ideas from passing *judgment* on them. Ask the groups to take two minutes to decide on the best one or two titles in their list. After they have decided, have the recorders present their selections. Then, if you wish, have the entire group try to pick out one or two of the best.

4. *Present another warm-up problem.* Go through the same procedure as was followed in the first one. A problem which is familiar to all should be used, such as "How can we keep roadsides free from empty beer cans?" or "How can we increase voter turn-out at the next election?"

5. *Present the main problem to be brainstormed.* Follow the same general plan as you used for the two warm-up problems, except give more time to the generation process. Try to maintain an atmosphere of friendly competition between the groups and continually challenge them to do better than the others in the room.

6. *Conduct or plan the final evaluation.* This evaluation process may be the same as was used in the introductory problems, or the cards may be collected from the recorders and turned over to a smaller group for evaluation at a more convenient time.

In summary, the conduct of this kind of meeting is very simple. The leader must be sure that the ground rules are understood; that the problem is stated clearly; that everyone is conditioned to present ideas; that the session is characterized by a free-wheeling, fast-moving succession of ideas, regardless of how foolish; that no one criticizes or comments; that all ideas are accepted as stated or as improved upon by a subsequent speaker; that a record is kept of everything; that the suggestions made in this session are evaluated; and finally, that a positive plan of action is adopted.

11

Role Playing

In recent years, role playing has become recognized as a group process in its own right. It simply calls for the unrehearsed acting out of a problem by members of a group so that it may be visualized and better understood by the group. It is used extensively by group leaders who want to add variety to their meetings and who appreciate the uniqueness of this action-oriented technique for getting people involved. It draws its value from the fact that many problems, especially those involving relationships between people, are not easily put into words. Words, furthermore, are not easy to remember. A dramatic or striking scene, on the other hand, may never be forgotten. It is especially effective when the situation being enacted deals with a problem that the group or a particular member or group of members must work out.

When should role playing be used? Two of the most common uses are:

1. Demonstrating techniques and training skills. People can be taught to do such things as selling tickets, soliciting donations, asking a person to join an organization, or presenting an idea to an important person or group (such as the boss or the Board of Directors).

2. Helping people understand feelings—both those of themselves and those feelings of others through having them switch roles and enact a situation in which they are involved with one another, and then describe to one another the feelings they experienced while in the other person's role.

An actual case in which this process was put to use may help to clarify just what it involves. A group of teachers were discussing some of their problems. One teacher came up with this: "Sometimes I want to get my students excused from other classes so we can take field trips to study places of interest. These opportunities often come up without much advance notice, and I have to go to my principal, say at nine o'clock in the morning, and try to get permission to take my students on a field trip that same day. How can I do this and still keep 'peace in the family'?" Questioning revealed the principal's characteristic attitude and usual reaction to requests of that kind. The leader then asked for a description of an actual situation and for two volunteers to act it out.

The group selected one person to play the part of the principal, who sat behind a desk at the front of the room. Another volunteered to be the teacher. He walked up to the front of the room, amicably greeted his fellow actor, and the show was on.

At first there were a few giggles and smart remarks from the audience, but soon everyone was attentive as the teacher made his pitch to get his students released from classes, and the principal raised objections. After three minutes or so, the leader told them to cut the action, and at that point the discussion *really* got under way.

Three minutes of seeing this scene acted out gave these teachers more tips on *what to do* and *what not to do* in a similar situation than any 30-minute discussion or lecture possibly could.

There seem to be two phases or parts to presenting a problem through role playing prior to the subsequent discussion.

● *A "warming-up" process* in which the problem is stated, the characters in the drama are described, the stage is set, and the actors are chosen. This should be done by the entire group, not by the leader alone.

● *The actual role playing* where the actors, drawn from the group, give their unrehearsed version of the situation.

During the discussion that follows the role-playing period, the group analyzes the action and the roles and draws conclusions on how to handle this and similar situations.

The potential uses of this device are many. It is particularly valuable in training people for public service and public contact jobs—teachers, salespersons, receptionists, clerks—a whole host of jobs. It is a real help in solving human relations problems of all kinds, as it portrays so well actions, expressions, feelings, and attitudes that *cannot* be described easily.

On another occasion, the membership of a group had dwindled to only 10 members. The situation was serious, and it was obvious that something had to be done to bring in an additional 10 or 15 new members. Various recruiting methods were considered, and it was decided to brainstorm desirable candidates for membership and then contact them personally. But what do you say to someone you hardly know? How do you get started?

The group decided to try role playing. One member volunteered to act the role of membership solicitor and another the prospective member. As the others watched, the recruiter went through the motions of knocking on a door, and the prospect responded by opening the door.

"Hi, Mr. Adams. I'm your neighbor Harvey Gersten. Do you have a few minutes?" (Adams welcomes Gersten into the house, and they sit down.)

"Steve, I belong to the 'Keep Morro Bay Beautiful Club,' and we've decided to extend our membership this year. I know you're pretty busy with your new store downtown, but membership in our club doesn't require much work. Would you be interested in joining?"

"Not really, Harvey. You see, we have two small children, and I like to spend as much time as I can with my family."

"Well, several of us have children too, and we plan special activities for families whenever we can. I'm sure you and your wife would enjoy meeting some of the families who belong to our club."

"No thanks, Harvey. When I get home from the store at night, I'm really beat. One more night meeting would be one too many! But thanks for asking me."

When a brief drama such as this one is over, the members all sit around and review what they have observed and make suggestions for improvement. As a group, they develop the best possible strategy for making direct contacts with selected prospective members and just how to get them to say "yes." Following are some additional suggestions for "directing" a role-playing scene.

Guidelines for Role Playing

1. Describe the situation. It should be familiar to all participants, and it should be clear, specific, and not too complicated.

2. Define the roles. Each person must know what behaviors and attitudes will be expected of him or her to play the roles.

3. Choose the actors. Volunteers are usually best, but they may also be appointed or recommended from sub-groups. *Never* select a person because he or she actually "fits" a particular role.

4. Set the stage. Keep the stage props simple. The "psychological stage" is much more important than having "things" in the proper place. Keep it simple. Explain the purpose of the role playing and the exact nature of the situation in focus.

5. Prepare the audience to observe. The audience should know what to look for. Sometimes it is useful to divide the audience into teams, with each team concentrating on a particular actor or looking for a certain behavior.

6. Enact the scene. Allow the actors a few moments to think over their parts. They should proceed spontaneously without script or notes. Stop the scene as soon as the main point has been sufficiently developed to form a basis for analysis and discussion. It should never take more than a few minutes.

7. Discuss and evaluate the role playing. Ask the role players to tell how they felt in their roles and how they reacted to the other characters in the drama. The audience or audience teams should also report their observations. Then the whole group should discuss the key points produced by the experience and develop ways to apply all of this to the real situation.

In summary, role playing can be a very effective way of preparing your membership for a lively discussion. Seeing a situation enacted, especially by your own members, gets everyone emotionally involved in a situation which, if presented by words alone, would be just another item on the agenda. Add it to your repertoire of ways to give variety and a change of pace to your meetings.

12

Special "Things"

Although *people* and the quality and variety of their interaction with one another provide the real substance of good meetings, there are "things" that can help make meetings go better. The effective use of speakers, panel discussions, symposiums, and forums (all discussed in Part 3) should be combined with the following "things" to provide you, the successful leader, with an excellent repertoire of activities for varied groups.

● *Videotape* is available to just about everyone through public or rental agencies, and the equipment is fairly easy to use after a few minutes of instruction. Since it is electronic rather than photographic, it gives you instant replay—over and over again if desired. Programs originated far away and long ago or in your own meeting room at that very moment can be experienced by your membership. What could be more entertaining or inspirational than to show some of your members preparing and serving a Thanksgiving dinner to crippled children, participating in a regional convention, or decorating a float for the annual parade? The scope of this particular "thing" is limited only by the range of your own imagination.

● *Movies* are a way of life for most of us, and movie-making is now simple and within the budget of anyone who enjoys it. The equipment to make movies and project them is compact, portable, reliable, and easy to operate. In addition, films on just about every subject are easily available and, if you own them, they can be edited easily for a particular purpose. A short film, selected to stress a point related to the next segment of the program, can be very effective in drawing the attention of your membership or audience to the subject at hand and in preparing them to be more active listeners and participants.

● *Slide shows* accompanied by either music (to create a feeling for the project at hand) or narration (either live or on tape), or both, can be a very effective and inexpensive means of presentation. The *purpose* behind your show must remain in the forefront of your thinking as you put it all together; and this exercise alone is an excellent one for the leader. And remember, **never use a media as a filler.** For as with all the components of your meetings, none should distract from your reason for being there.

● *Opaque projection* is an excellent way to show detailed information to a fairly large audience. Statistics, charts, and other ready-made material can be reflected on a screen from specially prepared sheets of paper or from magazines, books, or even photographs. The room must, however, be completely dark.

● *Overhead projection* has the advantages of being usable in a lighted room, and the speaker can face the audience while he or she is operating the projector. Since the light goes through a transparency to the screen, the speaker can have transparencies done in advance or write and create graphics in various colors while making the presentation. It is also a very useful way to list ideas from brainstorming (Chapter 10), arguments for and against an issue, or the names of people being nominated for office or named to a committee. It is an essential tool for large meetings when you want everyone to know, visually, what's going on.

● *Charts* of all kinds are very effective for relatively small groups. Charts can be pre-made with all sorts of colorful and exciting photographs and graphics, and the message of a speech or presentation will be better understood in less time than if you depend on words alone. And don't overlook the versatility of the velcro board. Before the meeting, take the time to set up your chart and back off from it to be certain that everyone can see the details. If the back row is too far away for people to see it easily, ask those in the back to move forward where they can see or take some extra time to explain the important details orally.

● **Newsprint pads** are many people's favorite! The message can be prepared in advance or recorded right on the spot. Buzz groups can work from their own pads, on an easel, or propped up against the back of a chair or a wall. Felt-tipped pens, chalk, and marking crayons can be used easily and are available in all colors. The results of work sessions can then be attached all over the walls of a room and provide for total recall of what's been done as well as be taken back to the office or home for future reference.

● **Live demonstrations** are always interesting and a welcome change of pace. They are, of course, somewhat limited to relatively small groups where everyone can see what is being demonstrated. Live demonstrations are hard to beat for programs presenting skills such as mouth-to-mouth resuscitation, flower arrangement, or water color painting.

● **"Hands-on things"** gives an extra dimension to some presentations. Passing things around to the members of the audience for them to experience through their senses of touch, smell, and taste will get them involved in what the speaker is saying. Examples of programs of this kind include such things as plans for landscaping a new building or park, the identification of different kinds of rocks in the area, plants or insects in mounted frames, and even cookies or candy made from seaweed or bees. When arrangements are being made for a speaker on a special-interest topic, use your imagination on how to expand the scope of the speech into a "hands-on" experience as well.

● **A pre-quiz** can probably be considered as a "thing," and while it may not sound too exciting, this technique can be very helpful in arousing membership interest in the program to follow. For example, a presentation on "Human Stress and How to Cope with It" may not be immediately stimulating, and some people feel they already know all about a particular subject. But a simple little well-designed quiz, one that will be done privately so as not to embarrass anyone, can get everyone personally involved with the subject even before the presentation. In fact, the quiz can be distributed early in the meeting for everyone to answer and ponder long before the program ever starts.

In summary, "things" make meetings more interesting, and some "things" are almost essential to effective communication. Used discriminately, the correctly selected "thing" will almost assuredly make meetings better. Take advantage of these when planning and setting a time schedule for your meeting. Try to weave these 10 "things" into as many presentations as you can, and get your team of helpers involved too.

Remember that "things," like people, have limitations. Take steps (literally!) to be sure that these "things" can be *seen and heard by everyone* in the audience. Check everything out in advance by walking to various parts of the room to experience the effects yourself, or have a member of your team do so for you.

Then, at your meeting, make sure to ask the members themselves, "Can you all see this chart from the back of the room? Can you all hear this OK?" For in the long-run, your *audience* should always be your main concern.

Part

3

The Formalities

Into the fabric of every organization is laced a pattern of meetings made up of committee reports, elections, and parliamentary procedure. These are the "formalities" of organizational life which accompany the tumult of internal change. And, for a little light and color, you might add an occasional speaker forum, a symposium, or a panel discussion.

Each of these formalities contributes something to the "personality" of the organization and deserves your total respect and your best effort as you plan for every meeting and program. And, they always seem to come out best when a leader shows both an awareness and an appreciation of the uniqueness of each person, as well as a competency in managing a variety of group techniques and processes. This all must be accomplished with a sensitivity to ever-changing situations.

Even when all this is done well, one thing stands above all the others in managing formal business. That one thing is **Teamwork**. No one person alone or even a small clique of persons, no matter how talented or clever, ever succeed in bringing an organization up to its full potential. This can be realized only through a spirit of working together—elected officers, appointed committee chairpersons, and volunteers alike. From the development of goals and the acceptance of roles to the rewards when the job's well done, a team will lighten the load and turn out a better product.

13

Club Meetings

You've just been elected by your fellow members to serve as their president. This is *your* year! Two of your many duties will be to preside at every meeting and to see that those meetings move right along as they should.

In many respects the meeting is the most important factor in the life of an organization: it's the one time each week (month) that the entire membership gets together to visit, to meet new members, to get the "big picture" of the organization, to hear reports on various projects, and to get involved in whatever is going on or being planned. It may be *the* most important hour of your organization week, every week!

Just about every club has certain things in common. The members are busy people, too, and there is a limited amount of time to spend fostering fellowship and boosting morale when people are eager to get everything said and done that should be. Here are some keys that may unlock the secrets of a really good meeting.

1. Have a plan and a timetable. While there are many variations in the general plans for meetings of different kinds of clubs, there should always be a plan—a logical sequence of things. Some service clubs start with a B-O-N-G on the bell; others with a gavel; still others with music, a prayer, a whistle, a clearing of the throat, "A-H-E-M!" Whatever the opening ceremony may be, the activities that follow can be quite varied, such as a call to order, the National Anthem, the Pledge of Allegiance, invocation, introductions, announcements, reports, business, speakers or special features, and finally, adjournment.

Luncheon or dinner meetings, of course, require the appropriate sequence of meal service, and some clubs rotate the leadership for the day. If business is to be transacted, the plan must include some of the features (parliamentary procedure, etc.) which will be discussed in this section.

Whatever you plan, it must fit into a timetable. Every club has certain limits on how long (or short) meetings should be. In order to make sure everything gets done, set a time frame for yourself for every meeting. Then when it's all over, review how well you did and adjust your plans accordingly for the next meeting.

It is especially important to make it clear to others who will be taking up time on the program just how much time they will have—then thank them after the meeting for keeping within that time allotment. Some people, you will learn, become oblivious to time passing when they have an audience. They may need special treatment, like loaning them your watch or seating someone alongside to tap them when their time is about up.

2. *Operate as a team.* Every club has a certain cluster of people with titles who have a portion of responsibility for the meeting: your vice chair, club secretary, and perhaps a sergeant-at-arms, program chair, host or hostess, music chair, or representatives of subgroups (or even "the central office"). Whatever the key positions are in your club, think of the people who fill them as your leadership team—and *use* them as such. Accept the fact that they can do some things better than you can; if these duties can be parcelled out to competent officers, you can give your attention to the "bigger picture" of what's going on.

Expect your team members to get to the meeting early, and be there yourself before they are. Review detailed plans for the meeting; and if there is a meal involved, you may, on occasion and when it is practical, want the whole team to eat in another place or behind the scenes before the others arrive (so you will all be free to give your full attention to the affairs of the meeting). Show them your plan and timetable and familiarize them with their part in it. Then when you call upon them to function, they will be ready without delay or confusion, and the meeting will move along smoothly.

3. *Promote friendliness by setting the pattern yourself.* Your attitude and what you do will generally set the tone for everyone else at the meeting. If you wish the members to greet guests and new or visiting members and make them feel at home, set the pattern for them. Those minutes when people are arriving should be time for socializing, a time for friendliness, with hand shaking and joyful conversation . . . for everyone, especially guests and new members.

If the leadership team has not "put it all together" before this, it will dampen this festive period because you and the other leaders will be "getting organized" among yourselves and missing out on this equally important activity.

4. *Keep things moving.* Two "sure-fire" ways of sabotaging club spirits are: (1) don't start meetings on time and (2) let meetings drag. Keep things moving! Your schedule and timetable will certainly help, and each part of the program should follow the one before it at a stimulating pace, not hurried, just brisk, crisp, and challenging.

Think ahead. Always know what you are going to say and do next. Be brief and to the point. Be alert. Keep your mind on your job. Watch for the reactions of the members. You can tell from what they are doing whether you are moving too quickly or too slowly. If they start looking at watches and whispering to others, speed things up. If they act confused and don't seem to be following what's happening, slow down a bit. Stick to your timetable and close on time. That's what they expect of you and you *can* do it.

5. *Give them a change of pace from meeting to meeting.* Nothing

can be quite so deadly and uninteresting to members as to be able to predict, before the meeting even starts, just what will happen from opening gong or gavel to adjournment. Give them some variety—something different every meeting.

Vary your method of introducing guests and visiting members from other clubs or chapters. It doesn't have to be done the same way every time. (See Chapter 15 for some guidelines.)

Encourage your members to suggest new ways to give variety to meetings, perhaps by visiting other clubs or chapters or by brainstorming it in small groups. If the ideas sound good, give them a try. It isn't necessary to change the overall standard pattern for your meeting; you can follow it and still introduce an interesting change of pace from time to time. And your group will probably be happy you did.

6. *Encourage member participation.* The way to get members to feel that a club or meeting is theirs is to make it so. Get everyone into the act if you can and see to it that he or she succeeds. This is the cornerstone of every successful club and of interesting meetings. Sure, this is your year, but you'd be foolish to try to do everything yourself.

7. *Know your organization.* Know the structure, purposes, functions, and policies of your club, and conduct your meetings accordingly. Every organization has certain guidelines, formal and informal, to give it continuity from year to year. Study them. They will add to your sense of security whether you are conducting a meeting of the executive board or presiding at a general membership meeting.

8. *Be yourself.* It's the only way that you can be at ease and natural. Your group elected *you* because you *are* you—not with the expectation that you should try to become like someone else. Smile, this isn't a very serious business, after all. Say "thank you," and let everyone know you mean it. This is *your* year.

14

Panel Discussions, Symposiums, & Forums

A **panel discussion** is a method of informing a group of persons regarding a subject by giving them an opportunity to hear the subject discussed informally by a smaller group. This small group or panel is generally made up of people whose wider knowledge and experience with the subject under discussion enables them to discuss it with some authority.

In reality it is an informal discussion held before an audience. Many so-called panels where several speakers present short talks are really *symposiums*. Handled correctly, the panel not only provides the audience an opportunity to listen to an informal discussion of a problem but also an opportunity to participate. Controversial issues lend themselves readily to this type of meeting, but informational subjects may be discussed with equal effectiveness.

The panel itself consists of from three to as many as six members and a discussion leader. They should be seated in a semi-circle facing the audience, with the leader at one end. *Don't line them up facing the audience;* they should be talking primarily to each other, not to the larger group. If a platform is available and sufficiently large to accommodate them, use it. It is important only that the audience is able to see everyone on the panel.

There is a practical limitation to the size of the audience before which a panel may perform effectively. Since the discussion is carried on in a conversational tone, the audience must be small enough and close enough to hear clearly. Perhaps 150 to 200 is the upper limit unless microphones are used by the panel.

The best way to describe how panels are planned and conducted may be to describe an actual program.

In this case the audience was about 100 high school and junior college teachers of farm mechanics—shop work. The subject was "What are the trends in farm mechanization, and what effect should these trends have on what we teach in our shops?" The general chairperson of the meeting selected and invited the panel members and the leader by letter, informing them of the subject, the names of the participants, the date, place, and other pertinent information. There were six panel members: two farmers who operated large, successful farms; two teachers of farm mechanics (one employed in a large high school, one in a junior college); one college instructor of agricultural engineering; and a research specialist employed by a county school system.

Thus, at least three points of view on this subject were represented: that of the farmer, the teacher, and the college professor. The research specialist was included because he had conducted a study of farms in the county and could provide pertinent facts. Because of his experience, he was cast in the role of fact-giver or resource person.

No further instructions other than the original letter and a copy of the overall program of the meeting were given the panel members until they arrived at the meeting. There the leader met with them for perhaps 5 to 10 minutes. He outlined his plan for the meeting. Briefly, it was this:

1. That he would ask two main questions:
   a. "What are the really significant things that are happening now in farm mechanization?"
   b. "As a result of these developments, what changes should be made in the content of shop courses for students who grow up on farms?"

2. That he would like to have them discuss these two questions informally; that no one would be expected to "make a speech."

3. That the college instructor take notes on the discussion and act as the summarizer.

These were the preliminary instructions given by the chairperson to the panel members and the discussion leader.

An hour and a half was allotted on the program for the discussion. Panel members were seated in a semi-circle on a low platform with the leader at one end. The program chairperson introduced the leader, and the leader conducted the discussion as follows:

1. He acknowledged the introduction and stated the subject. He had the members of the panel introduce themselves by saying, "Your chairperson has introduced me. Now I'm going to ask each member of the panel to stand, give his name, tell briefly what he does, what his job is, and why he feels competent to discuss these two questions. To start it off, I'll state my own qualifications. As the leader of a discussion, I don't need to know anything about the subject. I qualify fully in this regard. The gentlemen who *are* expected to know something about it will now introduce themselves, starting at the far end of the circle."

2. After the introductions, he stated the first question and let the panel discuss it for about 20 minutes.

3. He then asked for contributions from the audience as to trends not mentioned by the panel.

4. He asked the college instructor for the summary of the first part of the discussion.

5. Following the summary he introduced the second question (including changes indicated as a result of facts presented in the first part of the discussion).

6. After about 40 minutes, the audience was invited to ask questions and take part in the discussion.

7. The professor gave the final summary.

8. The leader closed the meeting by thanking the panel members and the audience for their contributions.

The elements that made this a success are easily identifiable and are basic to conducting effective panels:

1. The problem was an interesting one. It was meaningful and real to the audience. (The panel members were people who could speak with authority on the problem. They were known and respected. The two farmers managed 10,800- and 3,600-acre farms respectively. One employed 1,000 year-round farm hands. They *knew* what was happening on farms.)
2. They were conditioned to discussing the problem conversationally and informally. No one felt impelled to make a speech and no one did.
3. The members of the audience did not merely listen. They knew they would have a chance to take part and did participate in the discussion.
4. The leader simplified his job by briefing the panel members and the audience as to the plan of the meeting and by arranging for panel members to summarize. This left him free to give his full attention to keeping the discussion rolling.
5. The discussion was planned. The plan was simple, as most good plans are. It was merely:

This summarizes and illustrates the type of meeting where the *leader* formulates and states the problem to be discussed. Sometimes all that is given the panel leader is a subject or topic, and he or she is expected to draw out the statement of the problem or problems from the group.

This may be done in at least two ways. One very effective way would be to use the buzz session technique described in Chapter 9. To do this, the leader would state the subject, divide the audience into buzz groups, and ask each group to decide on the most important problem or problems that it would like to have the panel discuss. As the representative of each buzz group reports, the problems are recorded on a chalkboard or wall chart. Then either the panel or the audience decides upon the order in which the problems should be discussed, and the panel begins.

Another method would be for the leader to ask the panel members to state what *they* believe to be the most important problems suggested by this topic. These could also be recorded on the chalkboard or chart, then the audience members would select the ones they want to discuss.

Both of these methods provide more audience participation than the first one described, but they also take more time, so that at the end of the meeting a number of problems may have been identified but precious few of them settled. All, however, are good procedures to use, depending on what the situation dictates.

The Question Panel

In certain situations the "question panel" provides an interesting variation from the usual panel discussions and symposiums and is a most effective method of presenting certain kinds of information in a way that appears to be most interesting to audiences. Essentially it consists of having four or five people on the platform, who, under the guidance of a leader or panel moderator, respond to questions from a similar number of questioners. After some time is given for the responses to questions raised by panelists on the platform, the meeting may be thrown open to further questions from the audience. Formal presentations by either the questioners or the respondents are eliminated by having the respondents, prior to the meeting, submit prepared statements which are duplicated and placed in the hands of the questioners well in advance of the meeting and distributed to the audience sometime before the meeting begins. During the presentations, therefore, the respondents are called upon only to defend or to explain the position taken in the printed materials which are in the hands of the audience rather than to make formal presentations.

There are at least two kinds of situations in which this kind of presentation seems particularly appropriate: (1) those in which there are respondents who have achieved some distinction by having done some phase of their work exceptionally well and (2) those in which four or five people with different points of view on a specific subject have made their individual positions clear in brief written presentations and then have defended and explained their points of view in response to questions from the panelists and the audience.

In a successful question panel in which the author participated recently, three teachers, each of whom had done an outstanding piece of work in three different situations, were asked to submit briefs of their accomplishments several weeks prior to the meeting. These were duplicated and distributed to the audience 45 minutes prior to the time the panel was presented. The three questioners were supervisors and teacher educators and had received their copies earlier and so were able to prepare their questions well ahead of their appearance on the program. Questioners had been briefed and told that their questions should be almost entirely designed to bring from the respondents answers to the question "How did you do it?" The respondents had been informed that their answers should be limited to explanations of how they had obtained the positive results.

The physical arrangements for a panel of this kind are important. The respondents were seated at a long table facing the audience, the questioners at shorter tables at right angles to the one at which the respondents were seated. The seating arrangement, then, was a rather shallow "U" with the opening facing the audience.

The key factors for you as leader to follow for a successful question panel are:

1. *Using it appropriately.* Use this type of a presentation when you wish to have several people explain how they have accomplished a particular task successfully. Use it also when you wish to present several points of view or several positions on a specific topic and when you wish people who hold these points of view to have the opportunity to explain them and respond to questions about them. This device can be used to enlighten an audience about controversial issues.

2. *Selecting respondents.* Select people who have done some-

thing noteworthy, something in which the audience is interested; or people of some prominence who are noted for a particular point of view on some controversial issue.

3. Selecting questioners. Select questioners who are articulate and uninhibited; people who have enough knowledge of the subject under discussion that they are able and willing to ask intelligent questions.

4. Distributing written statements. Instruct the *respondents* to submit written briefs describing their accomplishments or points of view prior to the meeting. Have copies made, and present them to the *questioners* well enough in advance of the meeting to allow them ample time to prepare their questions. Distribute copies to the audience as far in advance as possible to give the *participants* an opportunity to read them and become familiar with them.

5. Arranging platform. Use one of the following platform arrangements: (1) two tables in the form of a "V" with the moderator at the apex, with questioners seated on one side of the "V," respondents on the other, and the open end of the "V" toward the audience; or (2) one long table at which the moderator and the respondents are seated with two shorter tables for the questioners forming a shallow "U" with the opening of the "U" toward the audience. When the audience is quite large, it may be necessary to have microphones available for everyone on the panel.

6. Introducing panel members. Have the leader of the panel briefly introduce the panel members. (This is possible since the written briefs contain the name, title, and address of each respondent.)

7. Initiating the session. Get the session started by a prearranged signal to the questioner who previously had been appointed to begin the questioning.

8. Calling for audience participation. After a 45-minute period of questions, answers, and discussion by the panel, allow a period for questions from the audience.

9. Summarizing. Have the panel leader summarize by capsuling the discussion personally, by asking one of the questioners to do so, or simply by asking for questions from the panel members which will lead them to summarize.

In summary, the leader must do these things for a successful panel discussion:

Before the meeting:

1. Plan and think through the procedure to be followed. Prepare a clear, interesting statement of the problem or problems to be discussed. Obtain written briefs from the respondents.

2. Brief the panel members and the panel leader prior to the meeting as to what to expect.

3. Check the physical arrangements and see that they are conducive to effective panel participation and audience comfort.

4. Arrange for summarizers and recorders for assistance, and have them distribute respondent briefs to the audience.

As the meeting begins and progresses:

1. Have the panel leader introduce the panel members.

2. Present the first problem.

3. Tell the audience members how and when they will have a chance to participate.

4. Have the panel leader lead the discussion—keep it going.

5. Have it summarized when appropriate.

6. Present other problems as time permits.

7. Call for audience participation.

As it closes:

1. Call for or give a final brief summary.

2. Thank panel members and the audience for their contributions.

Note again how the four basic precepts of effective group leadership are applied; how the leader must:

● Relax the panel (and the audience) and encourage them to take part.

- Become a member of the group.
- Give everyone something to think about.
- Help all members to help themselves.

The leader of the panel discussion then, becomes a medium through which both the panel and the audience think through a problem that is of concern to them.

Symposiums and Forums

A symposium-forum features a series of speakers discussing different aspects of a selected topic; a speaker-forum features a single speaker. Both are followed by interaction with the audience. These provide an interesting variation in club meetings. The key to excellence of a symposium or a forum is the amount of group participation generated between the speaker(s) and the audience. Without an interesting interchange with the audience, it is not much better than a series of lectures. Compared with a panel discussion, a symposium or forum is more formal and provides more information and instruction directly to the audience. These two techniques are also more suitable for larger audiences.

To insure a successful symposium:

1. Instruct the speakers to limit their formal talks to not more than *10 minutes* each (preferably 5) and see that they do.
2. Instruct them also to attempt to raise *questions* about the subject, rather than to try to give all the answers.
3. Use *buzz groups* to provide well-considered questions and contributions from the audience.

There are other techniques which will contribute to the general effectiveness of the meeting, but these three are the essentials.

The same general principles apply to conducting a forum. Naturally, since there is only one speaker, the speech may be longer, but it should not attempt to give all the answers, but should only point the way to interesting avenues for the audience to investigate and question.

Given an interesting subject, a speaker who does well will get a response from members of the audience without employing the buzz session. Too often, though, the results are pretty flat, and the silence that greets the leader when he or she asks "And now are there any questions you would like to ask Dr. Smith?" is too embarrassing to all concerned to chance it, especially when you don't have to.

A question box is a fairly good alternative to buzz groups. In this procedure, everyone in the audience is supplied with paper and is instructed to write out questions which he or she would like the speakers to answer. These are collected, read by the leader, and answered by the speaker to whom each is addressed. This lacks the spontaneity of questions coming directly from the group, but it does ensure there being questions to answer.

● *Remember: discussion is the key to planning and conducting a symposium.* The preliminary talks should merely set the stage, identify the problems, whet the appetites of the audience for the really important material of the program which comes after the speeches are finished. If this concept is rigidly followed in planning and conducting a symposium, it can be a highly effective and interesting technique to use. If not, well, you may have attended some . . . just another (ho-hum) meeting.

15

Speakers: Invitations & Introductions

The telephone rings at 1:15 Saturday afternoon. The voice at the other end says, "We'd like you to talk to our Rotary Club next Monday noon and tell us all about your recent trip to England. We meet in the Masonic Hall. Can you make it?"

Flattered and caught off guard, the sojourner answers, "Sure, I'll be there."

"Thanks," says the caller. "Click" goes the phone at the other end, and the deed is done. The odds are that the Millville Rotary Club won't consider that travelog the program of the year.

Let's consider the speaker first. The recipient of that type of call is really behind the proverbial "eight ball," whether he or she realizes it or not. Why? Well, here are a few questions that have to be answered: "What am I going to talk about? If I describe my whole trip and show the slides I have so carefully prepared for just such an occasion, it would take about two hours. How long should the talk be? What about the audience? Have any of them been to England? What are they interested in? Art? Business? Climate? The old buildings? What? Where is the Masonic Hall? Whom should I ask for at the door? Should I be there at 12:00 sharp, 11:45, or 12:15? Who else is going to talk? Am I the whole program? Will they want to ask questions? Should I allow time for that?"

In addition to all the things he or she *should* know and doesn't in order to give an effective talk, there is also the fact that there is very little time left to prepare the talk. What's the result? Probably a neurotic speaker and a bored audience.

To avoid all that when you're arranging for a speaker, do the following:

1. Contact your choice personally by phone or by letter at least two weeks in advance; longer, if the person is really important and may have other engagements. In any event, allow time for preparation.

2. Be specific about what you want the presentation to cover and suggest a title for the speech. "The Reaction of the British People to Socialism" or "The English Businessman," not "Tell us about your trip to England." Not only will a title give the speaker a lead and make his or her job easier, but also it will protect the audience from a vague rambling such as "We left New York Harbor on Monday and arrived in Blackpool. . . ," etc.

Just giving an interesting title to a talk can add that little extra measure of interest that makes the difference between a drab performance and a dazzling one. Consider these titles—"I May Be Wrong!," "Some of the Swans Are Swans," "It Can Happen Here!," "Our Inspiring Task." Don't they arouse your curiosity and make you want to hear what the speaker is going to say?

3. Give your guest some information about the audience—the number of people to be present, their interests, their ages, the occupations they represent. Give the speaker a chance to fit his or her remarks to your members.

4. Make clear the date, time, and place of the meeting; how to get there; who will meet and introduce the speaker. A person who doesn't know these things and is worrying about them while traveling to the appointment is hardly going to be in tip-top shape to give a dynamic address.

5. Specify the length of the talk and how much time the person should allow for questions.

6. Provide the names of the other speakers, their topics, and each person's place on the program.

7. Supply any other pertinent information about the room, the acoustics, facilities for projectors, etc.

Given this much information, the speaker is in a position to prepare and give a talk that will fit the occasion and the audience.

To make sure that there will be no forgetting or misunderstanding, confirm your invitation and the speaker's acceptance by letter.

The next time it falls to your lot to arrange for a speaker, do the things that have been outlined above, and both your speaker and your audience will bless you. Since it is easier to remember three or four things than seven or eight, probably the most important rules in inviting a speaker are these:

1. Extend the invitation long enough in advance to provide time for preparation.
2. Give the talk a title.
3. Identify the persons who will be the host and the introducer.
4. Confirm your invitation and the speaker's acceptance by letter.

Introducing a Speaker

There are probably more crimes committed by amateur MC's in making introductions than in any of the many other activities that take place in meetings.

Perhaps, the classic of classics is the introduction that allegedly was given the president of one of our better known universities. The president had received a letter from a former student asking if one of the professors could be obtained as a speaker and naming the subject. Recognizing the name of the writer and being interested in the subject, the president himself accepted the invitation. Overawed by the prestige of his speaker, the jittery alumnus started his introduction thus:

"Ladies and Gentlemen. We could have done with a poorer speaker than the one we got for tonight. In fact, we tried to get a worse one, but we couldn't!"

Some day a behavioral scientist will discover what it is that, when there are only two ways of doing even a simple job, the inexperienced person almost invariably chooses the wrong one. Perhaps it's the same thing that makes a piece of bread always fall butter-side down. In any event, introducing a speaker is so easy when done right that there is no excuse for doing it any other way.

Let's assume you have the job of introducing the president of the League of Women Voters. Here's what you should be trying to accomplish. First of all, you're selling her to the audience; selling her and what she has to say. Next, you are starting a process that a good speaker will continue the minute she starts to talk. You are getting her listeners interested and directing their attention to the speaker and her subject. Last, you are not only introducing her to the audience but also the audience to her, creating the kind of an atmosphere that will make the speaker want to put out and make the listeners receptive and at ease. You are paving the way for her and making the road easier. Keep in mind that you are not making a speech yourself; you are presenting the one who will do that job.

We said in the beginning that launching a speaker was so easy that there was no excuse for not doing it the right way. Here's the proof. You only have to remember to do these five things:

1. Just before the introduction, remind the speaker how long the talk should be.

2. Tell the audience briefly what the subject is and why the speaker is qualified to talk about it. Describe the title, position, or experience that gives the speaker authority. Don't give a complete biography, but hit the high spots.

3. Pronounce the speaker's name only once, as the final word of your introduction.

4. Lead the applause, and remain standing and looking at your guest until everything is set to go.

5. Then, and only then, sit down and congratulate yourself on a job correctly done.

It can be said that a good presiding officer knows the four "Be's":

1. **Be brief.**
2. **Be sincere.**
3. **Be enthusiastic.**
4. **Be seated.**

Let us analyze the five things which you should do in preparing the way for a speaker so that in addition to knowing *what* to do you will know why you are doing them.

Speakers seem to talk either far too long or not long enough. That's why it is absolutely essential that you impress on them just before they start that there is a time limit. Perhaps it would be well to point to your watch and say, "Look, it's just 8:35 right now. It'll be about 8:40 when you take the floor. These people expect you to talk exactly one hour; we want to be out of here at 9:45." That may sound pretty curt and you may be afraid of hurting your guest's feelings by being so candid in setting up such definite time lines. The most awful thing, though, is to have to sit through the rambling remarks of a speaker who has long ago worn out his or her welcome, the audience squirming in their seats, looking at their watches, and exhibiting all the symptoms of utter boredom. Spare your fingernails and your ulcers by making sure that this doesn't happen to you, knowing and appreciating that the brain can absorb only what the seat can endure.

Two objectives should be uppermost in your mind as you tell the audience about the speaker and the subject: (1) Sell the speaker and his or her subject to the listeners and (2) create suspense. In selling the speaker, be sincere but not sloppy. Emphasize what the person has done, the position held, his or her importance as a person and as a public figure, and the experience he or she has had in the field of the talk. The more important or well known a person is individually, the less you need to say and the less you *should* say. The perfect introduction for the man in the White House, then, would be, "Ladies and Gentlemen, The President of the United States." That is sufficient. More would be utterly superfluous and out of place.

Tell about the subject first and the speaker later. The sequence should be: *first the subject, next the person, last the name.* This serves as a natural build-up to create suspense. By describing the speaker, the position he or she holds, and the qualifications for speaking on the subject without indicating his or her identification, suspense is automatically created, and suspense builds interest.

The formality or lack of it in your manner while you are making an introduction will depend upon the occasion, how well you are acquainted with the speaker, and his or her prestige. A middle ground is the safest. Ponderous dignity, regardless of the occasion, is just as bad as launching the speaker by making him or her the butt of a joke. Humor is always good if it suits the occasion and if you can really use it effectively. Avoid it entirely if you can't. Nothing can be as flat as an allegedly funny story that doesn't make it. If you can tell stories well, and you know that the speaker is one who is alert enough to top you and take advantage of it, a joke on the speaker, well told, is a natural.

There may be occasions when it is permissible to mention the speaker's name before its logical place (your final and climactic word), but they are so few that you would do well to forget them. Just consider these two examples and contrast them in terms of the suspense and interest each would create.

1.

Ladies and Gentlemen: We are fortunate to have with us today Dr. Ruth Jones, noted authority on archeology, who is going to speak to us on the subject of "The Cliff Dwellers of the Southwest." Dr. Jones, as curator of the National Museum, has spent years exploring the ancient dwellings of the people who preceded us centuries ago in many states of the southern and western regions of our country. I'm sure many of you have read her books, and that you have been looking forward to the opportunity of seeing and hearing her in person. It is my pleasure to introduce to you Dr. Jones, noted author, scientist, and lecturer, who will speak to you now.

Not a bad introduction so far as the content is concerned, is it? But the sequence and the build-up are terrible. Now, suppose it had been said in this way:

2.

Ladies and Gentlemen: All around us here in the great

Southwest are the remains of homes and buildings left by the Cliff Dwellers who lived here thousands of years ago. Doubtless many of you have explored these remains or read about them and wondered what kind of people the Cliff Dwellers were, how they lived, what they did, how far their civilization progressed, and what happened to them. Today we have with us a woman who can give us the answers to these and many other questions about this ancient civilization which apparently disappeared so dramatically and mysteriously, a woman who has spent a lifetime studying these ancient people and telling their story in books and on the lecture platform. She brings us this fascinating story today, "The Cliff Dwellers of the Southwest." That noted scientist, author, and lecturer, the curator of the National Museum, Dr. Ruth Jones.

Don't you like the second one better? Notice the sequence and how the story progresses. First about the subject, next about the person, then why she speaks with authority, then specifically what her position is, and last her name.

Have you ever listened to the announcer at a prize fight introducing the principals and the visiting notables? His sequence is perfect. Tone down his inflection and the exaggerated emphasis on the name, and you've got the pattern down pat.

Now, after you've finished your introduction, continue your selling by what you do and how you do it. Start the applause. Remain standing and keep the applause going until the speaker is standing at the rostrum. Give and maintain the impression that you're presenting someone worthwhile. If you sit down and let the applause die, you say by your actions, "Well, here's your speaker. I hope you enjoy it but I have my doubts." Let there be no doubt in your words *or* your actions.

Now that you've been told what to do, here are some things to avoid. **These are the things you should never do:**

● *Never make a speech yourself.* You're the master of ceremonies, not the speaker. The main attraction follows you. Five minutes maximum should be your time limit, and the more you can cut that short, the better.
● *Avoid being too ponderous* and too dignified. Be natural, direct, brief; keep your introduction moving.

● *Don't overdo your enthusiasm.* Be sincere, and limit yourself to what you can say sincerely.

● *Avoid cliches,* especially, "The speaker we have with us today needs no introduction to this group." If he doesn't, what are you doing up there?

● *Don't talk about yourself.* You're not selling you, you're selling a speaker.

● *Don't tell jokes* unless you do it well and unless you're quite sure the speaker can top them or use them in starting his or her talk.

● *Don't let the name of the speaker slip out until you're ready for it.* Remember, that's the last thing you say.

● *Finally, never, never apologize for the speaker* who was sent to substitute for the one you hoped to have. It doesn't make any difference if Mr. Big has sent his seventh assistant to read Mr. Big's message; don't apologize. The most horrible introductions of all are those that begin, "I'm sure you are all as sorry as I am that the Governor was unable to be here and instead we have his secretary," etc.

Just keep in mind what your main objectives are in making introductions, and those do's and don'ts will all fall into their proper places. Remember:

1. You're selling the speaker and his or her speech to the audience.

2. You're getting the audience interested and attentive by creating suspense and building up to a climax.

3. You're creating an atmosphere that will put both speaker and audience in the proper mood.

4. You're doing this by being brief, sincere, and natural.

Using Speakers

While properly briefing the speaker beforehand and giving the right kind of an introduction are important factors in making the most effective use of speakers, there still remain some things to be done.

The most common error in arranging a program of any kind is to cram it too full. The most devastating situation speakers and any chairperson have to face are audiences who have sat through two hours of introductions, presentations of awards, speeches by practically everyone, and then (with the time all but gone) have to be the show of the evening. If you are planning the program, decide on what you think would be about right and then red pencil half of it. In any event, don't wear out your audience with a bunch of side-show attractions before producing your main event.

Sometimes a speaker is left with a let-down feeling after the speech is finished and the applause dies away. It is only ordinary politeness, of course, for you as chairperson to thank the speaker in behalf of the audience for taking the time to prepare and present his or her speech. However, if you really want to do the job right, take time when you get home or back to the office to write a personal note expressing your appreciation again and saying a few complimentary words about the talk.

16

Committees

Much of the business of a formal organization is done through committees. The excellence of the organization may very well depend more upon the success of its committees than upon its general meetings—although it's best to sacrifice neither for the other! It is safe to say, though, that you will seldom see a "top-notch" organization without an effective committee system. Let's look at five essentials to effective committees: *good members, good chairpersons, clear assignments, good plans of action,* and *good reporting plans.*

1. How to get good members. Be certain they are interested in the committee's assignment and that they are willing to spend the necessary time to get that job done in the time allotted. If special abilities are needed, be very clear about these qualifications when recruiting members. Have you ever noticed that some members tend to volunteer for just about every committee that comes along? This is common in every organization. But don't ask for volunteers. It may be the quickest way to form a committee, but it may also prove to be a "dud."

Here are some suggestions:

a. Let them know before they volunteer exactly what will be expected of them. The surest way is to write a job description in advance and give all members a copy or put it on a chalkboard or newsprint for all to see. If neither of the above is feasible, read the assignment to them from previously prepared notes. If none of these have been prepared, simply tell them.

b. Ask them to write on an individual piece of paper whether or not they would be willing to work on this committee, and if they are willing, what part of the task would they be most interested in doing. Be sure to ask them to print their name and give their telephone number. (Be prepared with paper and pencils for this technique.) When they have returned their papers, you can have either your vice president or the previously selected committee chairperson leave the meeting for a few minutes to study the results. Using the telephone as necessary, you can announce the committee membership before adjournment or between meetings. Another quick and effective way to get good committee members is to form buzz groups to get people talking about the committee's function and its importance to the organization. Then ask each group for suggestions—just as you would do in nominating people for office. (See next chapter.)

2. *How to select a good chairperson.* Finding someone who has time and a sincere commitment to the project or task of the committee should be only half of your concern. You are also looking for someone who can get the best performance out of others on the committee. We've all seen a project fail to meet expectations when one person, usually the chairperson, does all or most of the work while others either fail to show up or just go through the motions of being interested or busy.

Consider these two suggestions:

a. Call the first meeting of the committee yourself, after selecting the membership as suggested above, or ask your vice president to do so. Then lead an informal discussion about the committee's task and how it can best be accomplished. Get all members involved in the discussion, using every possible technique you know—buzz groups, brainstorming, role playing, etc. Finally, discuss whom they would like to chair *their* committee.

This process will come close to guaranteeing success. Not only will the committee have good members, but they also will have selected their own leader—someone they really want to work with. Team building and teamwork are already underway.

b. Select the chairperson in advance by considering all members you believe to have the necessary charisma to get people to work as well as those who have adequate knowledge of the task—people you can count on. (This is also an excellent way to give leadership experience to younger members who may some day be major officers in the organization themselves.) Talk to the person of your choice face to face, if possible, or on the telephone. In some instances, a well-written letter might be advisable to give him or her time to think about it.

When you have the best chairperson you can find, introduce him or her at the next meeting, along with a description of the committee's task. Then call for members as described earlier.

Getting members *after* the chairperson has been selected will bring forth not only those who want to help with this particular project but also those who really want to work with that particular chairperson. Again, if your membership is large, and some members are still a little shy, try buzz groups to come up with people who can be approached after the meeting or by telephone by the already selected chairperson.

This method of getting a chairperson is just about as effective as the first suggestion of having the members select their own. It gives you the opportunity to select the chairperson yourself . . . someone who will be a member of your overall organizational team.

3. *How to make the committee's assignment clear.* Just about anything can happen (and probably will!) when you form a committee and give it an ambiguous assignment. Perhaps you, too, have watched a major project bog down during debate on a motion. The all-too-common process goes like this: A member says, "I move we refer this to a committee." The motion is seconded

and, after brief discussion (if any), passed. The presiding officer says, "The motion is carried. Alice, you chair this committee and anyone interested should meet with Alice after the meeting." We have here an invitation to failure. Not only do we have an instant and poorly prepared chairperson but also a doubtful committee membership, all of whom may represent one point of view only. Furthermore, the task is nebulous. What in the world will this committee do, if anything? When and how will it do it? Alice will have to clarify the details later—not only who will be members but also what they are to do! This committee will need "lots of luck"!

If the matter is fairly simple or routine, of course, the presiding officer may dispense with it quickly: "This committee will conduct a telephone survey of the entire membership to determine whether we should increase our annual dues by $2.00 in order to publish and mail a monthly newsletter. The report will be given at our next regular meeting—February 14. Any questions? Hearing none, I will appoint and instruct the committee during the next couple of days."

If the project or problem is very important and/or complex, however, your procedures should be more thorough.

Consider these three suggestions:

a. Define the problem or task clearly before the meeting, then check it with your executive committee before presenting it to the whole organization. *At least*, check it with a few members in advance to be sure it really is clearly stated.

b. Present the problem to the membership at the next meeting and offer the opportunity to ask questions of clarification. Again, if the membership is too large or if some members are too shy, form buzz groups and interact only with the person in each buzz group selected as the group's representative.

c. When the committee is formed, tell its members what authority they have, such as spending money or taking action. "This committee will be expected to purchase an appropriate gift for our new chapter in Pozo and see that it is presented personally at its next meeting. The committee will also select a past president of our chapter who will be willing to make the trip and the presentation at no expense to the club."

4. How to develop an effective plan of action. The quality of the project and the solution to the problem will depend to a large extent on the quality of the action plan. The best path to quality is through the ideas of many, not just a few. How can we help the committee on this?

Here are some ideas:

a. Ask the membership. Brainstorm the project or problem. Do it at a regular meeting either directly with the chair or through buzz groups. "Our committee has a difficult job to do. Let's take a few minutes to help it." (When the committee is already formed, the membership is more likely to "loosen up." Some may not have wanted to be members of the committee for one reason or another, and talking too much too soon about the difficulty of the task could have caused this attitude.)

"How many ideas can we generate during the next five minutes that will help this committee do the best job for us? How should the members proceed? To whom should they talk? How should they organize themselves for best results?"

You'll be surprised and pleased at the number of good ideas that will emerge. The committee members will not only have the benefit of ideas but also the feeling that the organization really cares about how well they do.

b. For very difficult problems or goals, try the theory of Kurt Lewin's force field analysis.[1] It's really very simple and practical too. It is based on the fact that every goal exists in the midst of forces that affect its achievement.

Some forces are positive; that is, they are supportive and we can count on them to help us. For example: there may be a list of volunteers ready to assist; another club was able to do it

---

[1] Robert S. Fox *et al., Towards a Humane Society: Images of Potentiality,* NTL Learning Resources, Fairfax, Virginia, 1976.

successfully; certain needed resources are available; or if we can do this, we will be able to offer membership to physically-handicapped people in our neighborhood.

On the other hand, some forces are negative and will have to be overcome before the goal can be realized. For example: we may need a zoning variance from the planning commission; we don't have enough money in the treasury; or there will be considerable objection from people in the neighborhood.

After analyzing the positive and negative forces, weigh the whole matter to judge whether or not the goal is really worth the effort. The positive forces are motivational and offer promise of success, growth, and personal fulfillment. The negative forces, on the other hand, are challenges and barriers to the goal. Sometimes it may be an act of wisdom to drop this particular goal and to consider others with less formidable obstacles. Sometimes, however, the scales will tip the other way and a decision is made to go ahead . . . we'll do it!

Next, we consider each negative factor in terms of level of difficulty and develop a plan of action for each one. We can either develop plans for a single committee to overcome the various negative forces one at a time or set up several committees to work on them concurrently. Having the total membership brainstorm ideas on how to proceed is very much in order.

Each plan of action is stated as a problem: for example, "How can we obtain a zoning variation from the planning commission?" Follow the procedures for brainstorming stated earlier. Do this for each negative factor and agree on the date each will be overcome. Then, turn the brainstorming results over to subcommittees, select the leadership and a system of coordination, and bet your money on a successful project.

5. *How to get good reports.* The members must be kept informed of the results whenever they authorize a project or delegate a problem to a committee. Simple and routine reports are usually

done orally. Important and/or complex reports, however, are presented in writing and should contain certain basic elements.

Consider these six basics:

    a. The committee's assignment
    b. Methods used
    c. Work accomplished or information gathered
    d. Recommendations or resolutions
    e. The names of people or organizations that were especially helpful
    f. The names of committee members

Written committee reports can be handled in a number of different ways:

1. If the report is *adopted* or *accepted,* the organization agrees with its contents and is obligated to carry them out.

2. If the report is *filed,* the organization merely receives it as a matter of record without expressing approval, disapproval, or intentions.

3. Reports may also be *postponed, rejected,* or *referred* to an individual or another committee, or even *returned* to the committee for more information or additional work.

Committees are important in the life of all active organizations; they are essential to large organizations that function from brief infrequent meetings. In fact, in many large organizations all that is really accomplished is done by subgroups of the membership.

Committees offer these advantages:

    a. Members selected for their expertise.
    b. Meetings held oftener.
    c. Meetings conducted more informally.
    d. Decisions made more efficiently.
    e. Meetings isolated from the pressures and constraints of large audiences which tend to encourage a debating atmosphere for those who seem to thrive on rhetoric alone.
    f. Hearings held with outside experts and consultants as well as selected members of the organization.

g. Delicate matters handled privately to eliminate situations that would be awkward or embarrassing to deal with during a general session.

In summary, committees are important and often essential to organizations. They have several advantages over formal business meetings in thinking through problems and planning programs and projects. The presiding officer who wants to have a good term in office should remember:

GOOD COMMITTEES HAVE

GOOD MEMBERS
GOOD LEADERS
CLEAR ASSIGNMENTS
EFFECTIVE PLANS OF ACTION
GOOD REPORTING PLANS

17

Nominations, Elections, & Team Building

Changing officers is an annual affair for most groups and, like most things, there is a right and a wrong way to do it. One thing is certain: if it is done poorly, the chances of ending up with so-so officers are very good.

Selecting Nominees

Let's assume that you want officers who are: *interested, competent, dedicated,* and *charismatic.*

Not a shabby combination, is it? Actually getting people with these traits into office may seem a little naive, but not to try is contrary to the purpose of this book. We *must* try to get the *best* possible officers nominated and elected. But how do you find them?

Who Is Interested?

1. Ask. Obviously, this should be done before "opening the nominations" during a meeting. Talk to prospective candidates on the phone; write them a brief letter; make an appointment for this sole purpose; have lunch with them—there are any number of ways, but *ask them.* It's easy. "Charlie, we'll be electing new officers next month. Would you be interested in being nominated for the office of secretary?"

2. "Questionnaire" them. This can be done through the mail or at a meeting in just a few minutes. The questionnaire can be quite simple, for example:

LA PALOMA BIRDERS' CLUB

Leadership Search Questionnaire

We will be nominating officers at our next regular meeting on December 10, and this is your chance to indicate your interest in being on the ballot. If you check "yes" below, someone will call to make arrangements for your nomination. If you check "maybe," someone will call to answer any questions you may have.

There is also space below to indicate your interest in one of our major committees or any special project you would like to suggest. We do hope every member will be involved in some way during the coming year.

	Yes	Maybe	Comments
A. Are you interested in being nominated for:			
President			
Vice President			
Secretary			
Treasurer			
B. Are you interested in serving on the committee for:			
Publicity			
Program			
Field Trips			
Education			

C. Any other interests or suggestions: _____

_____

_____

Thank you!

Judy Purdy, President

The completed questionnaires can be considered by the executive committee before the next meeting or referred to the nominations committee (more on that later). If you must act on them at that very meeting (let's hope this never happens!), take the time to make certain that all persons interested in being nominated become well known to the membership. Ask them to describe to the membership their interest, qualifications, and dedication. Then form buzz groups, and rotate the various office-seekers from group to group so that every member has an opportunity to become acquainted with each of them personally.

Who Is Dedicated?

Dedicated officers are those who really believe in the club's objectives and somehow find the time to do the job. There are generally two methods to determine their level of dedication:

First, *listen to them:* People who believe in something talk about it, especially when they're interested in running for office. This is standard pre-campaign behavior. Most clubs give candidates the opportunity to "say a few words" before the members cast their ballots. This can also be done after members have shown their interest on the questionnaire and before opening the floor to nominations. One way to make sure they talk about their intentions to give the necessary time to do the job if elected is to give each candidate specific questions to respond to, such as:

● *How many hours per week would you give to the office, if elected?*
● *What other commitments do you have for next year that could compete for your time in this office (other than job and family)?*

Second, *look at past performance.* There is often a big gap between what a person says and what a person actually does. So try to get each candidate's "track record" out in the open with a couple more pertinent questions like:

● *What have you done for our club so far?*
● *What have you done as a member or officer of another group that would show that you really do get the job done?*

Who Is Competent?

Every office carries with it particular tasks or roles that require a degree of competence. Treasurers, for example, must be able to perform certain accountability procedures—receiving and depositing money, managing the petty cash fund, reconciling checks with bank statements, keeping a ledger, preparing purchase orders, making reports, preparing income tax statements, preparing budgets, and sometimes chairing the finance committee. These are critical skills to consider in nominating and electing a treasurer. A list of necessary competencies should be prepared for every office.

But how can we learn these things about people *before* they are nominated? Some of the following ideas may work for your organization:

1. Make a list of competencies for each office and distribute it to all members, along with the questionnaire illustrated earlier.

2. Have the outgoing officers give a brief talk about the skill requirements of their individual positions before nominations are open or the questionnaire is distributed.

Identifying Charisma

Don't confuse charisma with "political charm" or highly polished social skills. Charisma is an inner strength defined in dictionaries as "personal power belonging to those exceptional individuals capable of securing the allegiance of large numbers of people." Granted, we may not need a Messiah to preside over every group. It would be a step in the right direction, however, if we had leaders with respect for all members and the power to bring out their best effort in the pursuit of organizational goals. As a general rule, the better we know one another personally, the more likely it is that charismatic leadership will be easily identified within the membership.

Chapter 6, "Getting People Acquainted," suggests five ways of getting people to know one another. Lawson,[1] in *Leadership Is Everybody's Business,* offers nine additional methods of getting people acquainted through structured interaction games.

Using a Nominating Committee

All of the above procedures will help get good people on the ballot. However, these things don't "just happen," but a dedicated nominating committee will make them happen.

● A nominating committee, properly instructed, can see that the procedures you choose to use actually do happen.

● A nominating committee can coordinate the whole process of recruiting interested, competent, dedicated, charismatic members who will accept nomination.

● A nominating committee can match the competencies of individuals with the requirements of each office.

● A nominating committee can put together a list of nominees who will work together harmoniously.

● A nominating committee can present a slate that is representative of the entire membership.

● A nominating committee should select *the* best candidate for each office, not two or three for each office. There is no particular joy in being defeated in an election, even among friends. Furthermore, additional nominees can be added from the floor when the committee's report is presented.

● A nominating committee can nominate a member of the committee for an office—a perfectly proper procedure; if this were not permissible, some excellent candidates might be omitted.

---

[1] John D. Lawson, Leslie J. Griffin, Randy D. Donant, *Leadership Is Everybody's Business,* Impact Publishers, Inc., San Luis Obispo, California, 1976.

Selecting a Nominating Committee

This particular committee should be *elected* by the membership rather than *filled* by volunteers, *appointed* by the president, or *selected* by the executive committee. To some, this election may appear to be an unnecessary extra step, but it *is* the most democratic method. An elected committee will "guarantee" a committee representative of the membership, and it is more likely to prepare a list of nominees representative of the membership. It also avoids the problem of some members' feeling the organization is being run by a clique.

Conducting a Meeting During Nominations

The nominating committee report is read by the chairperson of the committee to the membership, then handed to the secretary. The presiding officer presents the candidates for one office at a time as follows: "Joan has been nominated for president. Are there any further nominations?" If there are, ask the person named if he or she accepts the nomination. There is no need to "second the nomination"; this is appropriate only for the purpose of making a brief speech in support of a candidate, usually during the meeting when the election is held. When there are no further nominations for an office, just move on to the next. There is no need to have a motion "to close the nominations." The presiding officer simply states, "Since there are no further nominations for vice president, the nominations are closed."

Conducting the Election

When there are two or more candidates for an office, it may be desirable to complete the nominations during one meeting and hold the election at the next meeting. The organization's bylaws generally indicate how this must be done.

In any event, elections are held by voice vote, hand vote, standing vote, or ballot. Prior to voting, it is helpful to give each candidate an opportunity to make a brief statement, and when there are more than one candidate for an office, to accept comments from other members who would like to speak in behalf of a particular candidate.

Some organizations nominate and elect officers for one position before moving on to the next position. This method is defended on the grounds that the person defeated for president would make an excellent vice president and so on down the line. It is more likely that a group of officers, some of whom have been defeated by others for an office they would rather have held, do not make for the best possible team during the year ahead. It also violates the very important principle of electing candidates for their particular competencies.

The vote necessary to elect a candidate to office is generally stated in the bylaws. A *majority* is defined as "at least one more than half of those voting," a *plurality* as "most votes received by any candidate." A simple majority vote is required whenever no special bylaws provision is made for plurality. Whenever there are three or more candidates and no one candidate receives a majority, it is common practice to conduct a *run-off* between the two top vote-getters. Write-in candidates are permitted in the original, *general* election, but a run-off is a *special* election between two favorite candidates. Furthermore, one or more write-in candidates could conceivably prevent either of them from getting a majority—over and over again.

A motion to result in a unanimous vote, or *white ballot*, for the winning candidate is sometimes made to show the organization's total support to the winner. This may do something for the morale and good will of the overall membership, but it does not change the *legal* vote which is entered in the record books.

Vacancies should be filled as soon as possible, and procedures for this are frequently stated in the bylaws. Elections to fill vacancies may be held at any special or regular meeting unless the bylaws specify other methods. The earlier discussion about a nominating committee procedure and getting interested, dedicated, competent, charismatic nominees is still valid.

Transferring Responsibility

The transfer of responsibility *between* officers *after* an election is a critical procedure in the life of an organization, and it should be done systematically at a special session with all outgoing and incoming officers present.

Some organizations traditionally do this informally between sets of two individuals involved with each office and at their personal convenience. The thoroughness of this method and whether or not it is done at all is unknown to the other officers.

It is much more valuable for all newly elected officers to experience this transfer together at a special session as one large group. One outgoing officer at a time transfers his or her paraphernalia to the newly elected officer and offers suggestions about how to get the job done most effectively. For example, Clyde, the outgoing secretary, might say: "Leonard, the job of secretary is a lot of work and I have found it very helpful to have some assistance in getting the minutes typed, duplicated, and mailed. Roscoe and Bob were especially helpful with the typing and duplication. Stop in at the post office to see George about the status of our special mailing permit. And, oh yes, be sure and give all your receipts to our treasurer. Here is a complete set of last year's minutes and correspondence. Wilbur, our faithful historian, has all the earlier records." And the transfer continues with recommendations and questions, the other officers listening and sometimes participating themselves.

When each set of officers has done this, with the others observing and helping, every new officer gets a rather complete understanding of the need to work together and function as a team.

Team Building

A team is more than a collection of individuals, each carrying out a given role. And the proper development of a team from the officer group is an important task. The team is a group of individuals, each doing a certain specific task in coordination with every other individual, and always toward a common goal. In many ways, it is similar to a baseball team where each player takes care of his or her own position and knows what every other player's job is too. No one functions independently; signals are constantly being shared to take advantage of every opportunity to achieve the team's goal—making runs and keeping the other team from doing the same. A "pick-off" play at second base involves more than one or two players. The whole team reacts promptly to every opportunity or threat with advance knowledge of each other's anticipated action.

Team members observe each other and talk among themselves about how to improve. They are not totally independent. Nor are they totally dependent, for that too would weaken the team. They are interdependent, working together, not *for* one person, not even for each other because they are working for themselves too . . . they are interdependently working toward a common goal. This relationship and attitude is just as important in your organization as it is within a baseball team.

A common problem with an organization's leadership being made up of volunteers is the belief that some of the officers are more important or even better than other officers and members. This is damaging to the concept of teamwork, where everyone is equal—everyone just has a different role to play. Only you, the presiding officer, can set this straight by your own behavior.

Have you ever seen a president step in and do the job of someone else because "it wasn't being done right?" Sure you have. And you've probably seen a president "chew out" another officer for not having done something just the way the president wanted it done. Neither of these is appropriate in an interdependent team of equals!

The first step toward team building is for the officers to become acquainted with one another on a personal basis. There's more to it than seeing each other at executive committee sessions between meetings. Try one of the several methods suggested in Chapter 1, and don't be afraid to invent variations to fit your particular group. Try having a special get-together just to get acquainted—with no business to transact. Remember, a winning baseball team spends a lot of time together between games—even before playing the first game.

Another important step which should be taken early is for each officer to become acquainted with the bylaws and what they tell about the group's general goals and operations. In some organizations it is not uncommon for an officer to go through a whole year without ever seeing the bylaws! Even though this may have been discussed with the outgoing officers, it's important to do this thoroughly among themselves without others present. It's also not uncommon to find the older officers doing most of the talking and advising at the joint session. Now that the out-going officers have stepped out of the picture, the new team can do it on its own.

When each officer is discussing his or her own role, it is an opportune time to suggest that each also talk about any personal goals he or she may have while in that office. The whole team should join in and offer ideas on how these personal goals can be achieved.

Beyond personal goals to carry out the duties of each office, the team should consider goals for the organization as a whole. A review of Chapter 8 will remind you to keep these decisions on organization goals very tentative if you expect to get maximum participation from the general membership. Discuss them? Yes. Tentative plans? Yes. Final decisions? No!

As a final step in getting the team ready for the new year, take a look at your resources, not only available cash, supplies, and equipment but also people and groups that you can count on. If your organization has employees or advisers, invite them to hear your tentative plans and ask for their advice. If you are a chapter or affiliate of a larger organization, review the documents, make some telephone calls, or write some letters to become totally informed about what your affiliate can do to help you. And finally, inventory your neighborhood and community, its organizations, businesses, and public agencies. Check them all out before your year in office starts; they are all a part of your group's total resources.

With the nomination and election of new officers who are interested, competent, dedicated, and charismatic, and with a well-planned team-building experience, together with an inventory of available resources, your year as presiding officer will be off to an excellent start.

18

Parliamentary Procedure Made Easy

When someone in the membership says, "Point of order," "I move the previous question," or "I rise to a question of privilege," many presiding officers literally panic or reach for the parliamentarian as a drowning person would reach for a life ring. From the other side of the rostrum, members who know very little about the jargon of "parly pro" often drop out of participation in the meeting because they just don't know this special dialect of the English language.

Neither panic nor dropping out is necessary. Parliamentary procedure is easy. It is based on seven very simple and democratic principles.

1. Its purpose is to facilitate business and to promote cooperation and harmony.

2. All members have equal rights, privileges, and obligations.

3. The majority vote rules.

4. The rights of the minority must be protected.

5. The membership must have full and free discussion of every proposal.

6. Every member has the right to know the meaning of a question and what its effect will be.

7. All meetings must be characterized by fairness and by good faith.

Order of Precedence	Can Interrupt Speaker?	Requires a Second?	Debat-able?	Amend-able?
I. PRIVILEGED MOTIONS				
1. Adjourn	no	yes	no	no
2. Recess	no	yes	no	yes[2]
3. Question of privilege	yes	no	no	no
II. SUBSIDIARY MOTIONS				
4. Postpone temporarily (lay on the table)	no	yes	no	no
5. Vote immediately (previous question)	no	yes	no	no
6. Limit debate	no	yes	no	yes[2]
7. Postpone definitely	no	yes	yes[2]	yes[2]
8. Refer to committee	no	yes	yes[2]	yes[2]
9. Amend	no	yes	yes	yes
10. Postpone indefinitely	no	yes	yes	no
III. MAIN MOTIONS				
11. (a) A General main motion	no	yes	yes	yes
(b) Specific main motions Reconsider	yes	yes	yes	no
Rescind	no	yes	yes	no
Resume consideration	no	yes	no	no
Create orders	no	yes	yes[2]	yes[2]
IV. INCIDENTAL MOTIONS[1]				
Appeal	yes	yes	yes	no
Point of order	yes	no	no	no
Parliamentary inquiry	yes	no	no	no
Withdraw a motion	no	no	no	no
Suspend rules	no	yes	no	no
Object to consideration	yes	yes	no	no
Division of a question	no	no	no	no
Division of assembly	yes	no	no	no

[1]No order of precedence among themselves. Each motion decided immediately.
[2]Restricted.
[3]After change in parliamentary situation.

GOVERNING MOTIONS

Vote Required?	Applied to What Motions?	Motions Can Have What Applied to Them (in Addition to Withdrawal)?	Can Be Renewed?
majority	no other motion	no other motion	yes[3]
majority	no other motion	amend[2]	yes[3]
no vote	no other motion	no other motion	no
majority	main, amend, appeal	no other motion	yes[3]
two-thirds	debatable motions	no other motion	yes[3]
two-thirds	debatable motions	amend[2]	yes[3]
majority	main motion	amend[2], vote immediately, limit debate	yes[3]
majority	main, amend	vote immediately, limit debate	yes[3]
majority	variable in form	subsidiary motions, reconsider	no
majority	main motion	vote immediately, limit debate	no
majority	no motion	specific main, subsidiary object to consideration	no
majority	main, amend, appeal	vote immediately, limit debate, postpone definitely	no
majority	main motion	all subsidiary motions	no
majority	main, amend, appeal	no other motion	yes[3]
majority	main motion	amend	yes[3]
tie or majority	decisions of chair	limit debate, vote immediately postpone temporarily or definitely	no
no vote	any error	no other motion	no
no vote	no motion	no other motion	no
no vote	all motions	none	yes[3]
two-thirds	no motion	no other motion	yes[3]
two-thirds negative	main motion	no other motion	no
no vote	main, amend	no other motion	no
no vote	voices votes	no other motion	

(Source: Alice Sturgis, *Sturgis Standard Code of Parliamentary Procedure*, 2nd edition, McGraw-Hill Book Company, New York, New York, 1966.)

When in doubt about any particular parliamentary situation, you should be guided by these basic principles.

Parliamentary procedure, like any body of knowledge (or any skill), takes both study and practice. If you find *Robert's Rules of Order*[1] confusing, purchase a simplified and condensed version for each reference. Or try *Sturgis Standard Code of Parliamentary Procedure*.[2] It emphasizes simple language; it is organized for each reference; it is based upon court decisions and legal research; and it is kept current by a permanent board of more than 30 nationally recognized parliamentarians. Sturgis also authored *Learning Parliamentary Procedure*,[3] a learn-it-yourself book. Whatever you do, be prepared by self-study and by practice. And whatever you do, **do not bluff!** Use your parliamentarian, even declare a brief recess to think your way out of a confusing situation, but don't "fake it."

This book is not meant to be a substitute for a basic reference on the many details of formal parliamentary procedure. It will, however, clarify the most common situations that you will experience.

Let's start with some fundamentals:

● *What do you do with the gavel?* One rap of the gavel simply means you have made a decision. An example would be to rap once immediately after you announce the motion is carried or defeated. Two raps means "Please rise," *or* "Please be seated." For example, two raps signifies that it is time to rise to salute the flag, time to rise for prayer, or time to rise for a moment of silence, at the end of which two raps signifies that it is time to be seated. Three (or more) raps means "Come to order," usually to begin a meeting, to get things started again after a recess, or even to get the attention of buzz groups. To call the meeting to order, rap the gavel three (or more) times and say, "This meeting will come to order," *or* "This meeting is now in session" (or whatever is traditional for your organization).

---

[1] Henry M. Robert, *Robert's Rules of Order*, Scott, Foresman and Company, Atlanta, Georgia, 1921.

[2] Alice Sturgis, *Sturgis Standard Code of Parliamentary Procedure*, 2nd edition, McGraw-Hill Book Company, New York, New York, 1966.

[3] Alice Sturgis, *Learning Parliamentary Procedure*, McGraw-Hill Book Company, New York, New York, 1953.

A Matter of Precedence

The table on pages 146 and 147 displays the order of precedence of 11 motions and a summary of the principal rules governing motions. It also lists eight incidental motions which have no order of precedence. You will note a definite and logical listing which governs the order of making and handling all motions. It is necessary to give the more important ones a priority or precedence over those less important. Properly handled, there will be only one motion on the floor being discussed at once and that motion will be managed in the light of the urgency or precedence of all others.

● *Main motions* make up the principal business of a meeting. All other motions are generated from these, so main motions have the lowest level of precedence. They are simply the "bottom line" of all parliamentary actions.

● *Subsidiary motions* offer seven alternatives for changing or disposing of the main motion.

● *Incidental motions* arise incidentally from the business of the organization and are not ranked. They are concerned with the rights and privileges of members.

● *Privileged motions* are really main motions which are handled with urgency because they must be decided before the question on the floor.

It is best *not* to memorize the precedence of the 11 primary motions of parliamentary procedure. Experience will soon fix their rank in your memory because of the logic of their precedence.

There are two general rules of precedence:

1. When a motion is on the floor, any motion of higher rank may be proposed, but not motions of lower rank.

2. Motions are considered and voted on in the reverse order of their being proposed.

Handling a Main Motion

Have you ever seen someone at a meeting just start talking about a problem and go on and on about it? It happens all the time, especially in groups that have not yet learned that this sort of "freedom of speech" is not what democracy is all about.

Parliamentary procedure requires that a member state a proposal for discussion clearly and concisely to see if another member also wants to have that proposal placed before the membership for consideration; it also requires that it be stated in the affirmative. That is called making a motion and getting a record. It goes like this:

> **M[4]:** *(After getting recognition from the presiding officer)* "I move that we go on record as favoring the new school bonds."
>
> **AM:** "I second the motion."
>
> **PO:** "It has been moved and seconded that we go on record as favoring the new school bonds. Is there any discussion?"
>
> **M:** *(After getting recognition from the presiding officer)* "I am in favor of this motion because . . ." *(The maker of the motion should be recognized first because the membership has not yet heard from the member who initially wanted this discussed.)*
>
> **AM:** "I am opposed to this motion because . . ."

When all points have been made favoring and opposing the motion or there is a lull in the discussion, ask, "Are you ready for the question?" Then call for the vote.

> **PO:** "It has been moved and seconded that we go on record as favoring the new school bonds." *(Repeat the motion just before voting.)*
> "All in favor, say 'aye' (pause)."
> "All opposed, say 'nay' (pause)."
> "The motion is passed (or defeated)." *(Rap the gavel once.)*

Always give equal instruction/direction to those who want to vote in favor of the motion and to those who want to vote against a motion. For example, it is *not* equal to say, "All in favor, say 'aye'; all those opposed (pause)."

---

[4]Throughout the next few pages you will find the following abbreviations: M = Member; AM = Another Member; PO = Presiding Officer.

Whenever the vote required is two-thirds, state the exact vote to the membership and have it recorded in the minutes. "The motion passes by a vote of 34 to 17," *or* "The motion is defeated by a vote of 33 to 18."

Reconsidering and Rescinding Previous Action

An action at one meeting can be reconsidered at that same meeting. If it involves a later meeting, the proper motion is to rescind, which means to repeal or cancel an action previously taken.

Reconsider

M: "I move to reconsider the vote by which the motion to increase our dues was passed earlier this evening."

AM: "I second the motion."

PO: "It has been moved and seconded to reconsider the vote by which the motion to increase our dues was passed earlier this evening. Will the secretary please read that motion? . . . Thank you. Is there any discussion on the motion to reconsider this vote? . . . Those in favor of reconsidering the vote, say 'aye' (pause); those opposed to reconsidering the vote, say 'nay' (pause); the motion to reconsider is carried. The motion to increase our dues as read by the secretary is again open for discussion."

Rescind

M: "I move to rescind the motion passed at the meeting on June 10 opposing a new municipal swimming pool."

AM: "I second the motion."

PO: "It has been moved and seconded to rescind the motion passed June 10 opposing a new municipal swimming pool. The secretary will please read the motion referred to. . . . Thank you. Is there any discussion? . . . Those in favor of rescinding the motion read by the secretary, say 'aye' (pause); those opposed to this motion, please say 'nay' (pause); the motion to rescind is carried. The motion that this organization go on record as opposed to a new municipal swimming pool is rescinded."

Adjourning a Meeting

This procedure is similar to recessing. "I move that we adjourn." The motion is seconded and voted on *without* discussion. A meeting in less formal organizations can be adjourned by the presiding officer unless there is an objection, in which case there must be a vote. You cannot adjourn a meeting on your own since the meeting is really a meeting of, for, and by the membership, just like the language of the U.S. Constitution.

There's one interesting point, however. You have the authority to delay the vote on the motion to adjourn if adjournment, in your judgment, is premature. In this case, it is proper for you to inform the membership of important business that should be transacted before adjournment. Important announcements should also be accepted before you say, "This meeting is adjourned," and rap the gavel once indicating your decision.

Declaring a Recess

This is a decision the membership must make. It is technically out of order for you to declare a recess without membership approval. To put the motion in its most formal form, a member states, "I move we recess for 10 minutes" (*or* "until tomorrow morning at 10 o'clock," *or* "until the next regular meeting," or any number of similar conditions). The motion is seconded, discussed *very briefly*, if at all, and voted on. You follow with, "This meeting is recessed until . . ." *or* "The motion is defeated and we will continue with the meeting . . . ," etc.

In less formal situations, after a motion is made to recess, you can ask, "Are there any objections to recessing at this time until . . . ?" "Since there are no objections, this meeting is recessed until. . . ."

It is not uncommon in some organizations for the presiding officer to declare a recess without a motion or permission from the membership. This is really not proper unless this authority is stipulated in the bylaws or standing rules of the organization.

Questions of Privilege

Questions of privilege enjoy a very high ranking in the order of business because they involve such matters as the rights, privileges, and comforts of the membership. These "questions" need not have any direct connection with any other business before the assembly. They involve a certain privileged urgency that requires an immediate decision and action by the presiding officer. These privileged procedures can be presented in one of the following three ways:

1. Question of Privilege of the Assembly

M: "I rise to a question of personal privilege of the assembly."

PO: "State your question of privilege."

M: "May we have the amplification increased so that we can hear in the back of the room?"

PO: "Your request is granted. Will the technician please turn the sound up a little?"

2. Question of Personal Privilege

M: "I rise to a question of personal privilege."

PO: "State your question of privilege."

M: "May I have Mr. Robert Brown cast my ballot during the remainder of this convention? I must return to my office immediately."

PO: "Your privilege is granted."

3. Motion of Privilege

M: "I rise to a question of privilege to present a motion."

PO: "State your motion."

M: "As a motion of privilege, I move that the newsletter editor by directed to list the names and addresses of all present at this convention in the next edition."

AM: "I second the motion."

PO: "As motion of privilege, it has been moved and seconded that the newsletter editor be directed to list the names and addresses of all present at this convention in the next edition. It is the opinion of the chair that this matter can be discussed directly with the editor and does not require interrupting the business now being discussed. We will continue discussion on the question, which is . . ."

(Motions of privilege are for matters of urgency only. The chair must decide each motion of privilege on its own merit as it relates to the current situation.)

Postponing a Motion

Often it is desirable to postpone a motion temporarily, to a definite time, or indefinitely. Let's consider them one at a time.

Temporary postponement is done within the time of a single meeting. *Robert's* calls this "laying it on the table." It is simply setting aside the current discussion until a motion is passed to resume consideration of that question. This motion is common when more urgent business has arisen, or when members want additional information or more time before voting.

M: "I move we postpone this matter temporarily."

AM: "I second the motion."

PO: "It has been moved and seconded to postpone this question temporarily." *(There can be no discussion.)* "All those in favor, please say 'aye' . . . ," etc.

A motion which has been postponed temporarily is terminated if it is not resumed by a motion to resume consideration at that same meeting (*Robert's* calls this "taking from the table.")

Postponement to a definite time is very common.

> **M:** "I move to postpone definitely this matter until we have heard the audit report," *or* ". . . until the next meeting or convention."
>
> **AM:** "I second the motion."
>
> **PO:** "It has been moved and seconded to postpone definitely this matter until the next meeting. Is there *brief discussion* about the time or reason for postponement?"

Indefinite postponement is proposed to further present discussion or a vote on the main motion. In effect, it is meant to terminate any further action on the main motion during that meeting or convention. An interesting parliamentary gimmick is that this powerful motion requires only a simple majority vote.

> **M:** "I move that this matter be postponed indefinitely."
>
> **AM:** "I second the motion."
>
> **PO:** "It has been moved and seconded to postpone this matter indefinitely. Is there any discussion on this motion or the main motion?

(Note that both the motion to postpone indefinitely and the main motion are open to debate at the same time.)

Referring a Motion

Referring a motion is simply a transfer of business to a committee.

> **M:** "I move to refer the question to a committee."
>
> **AM:** "I second the motion.
>
> **PO:** "It has been moved and seconded to refer the question to a committee. Is there any discussion?"

Sometimes this motion will specify the number of committee members, how they shall be selected, who the chairperson shall be, even special instructions as to how to proceed and when to report. If the motion does not specify these details, the presiding officer must take the initiative to do it immediately after the motion is passed or at a later time. These specifics can also be handled through amendments during discussion of the motion.

Amending a Motion

Main motions can be amended at any time to express the will of the members more satisfactorily. The maker of a main motion can, of course, change the wording of a motion until the time the presiding officer presents it to the membership for discussion. It is also your responsibility as presiding officer to assist the maker of a motion with the wording so that it will be clear, concise, and stated in the affirmative before being presented to the membership.

● *Informal "friendly" amendments* often can be handled more simply and quickly than through formal procedures. During discussions of a main motion, a member may say, "I move the following as a friendly amendment: . . ." The presiding officer addresses the membership with, "Is there any objection to amending the main motion so that it would read . . . ?" "Seeing none, the question now reads . . . ," *or* "Since an objection has been raised to this friendly amendment, the chair will accept a motion to amend."

● *Formal amendments* generally involve one of three changes: the addition of words, the deletion of words, or a combination of striking out certain words and adding others.

Let's suppose the following main motion is being discussed:

"That we send representatives to the Board of Supervisors and the County Planning Commission to express the need for a new park system."

> *Examples:* 1. *Addition of words.*
> "I move to amend the motion by inserting the word 'three' before the word 'representatives.'"
> 2. *Deletion of words.*
> "I move to amend the motion by deleting the words 'to the Board of Supervisors.'"

3. *Combination of above.*

"I move to amend by striking out the word 'representatives' and inserting the words 'the executive committee.'"

In every case, you should not only repeat the motion to amend but also state how the main motion would read if the proposed amendment carried. For instance, in the third example you would say, "It has been moved and seconded to amend the question by striking out the word 'representatives' and inserting the words 'the executive committee' so that, if passed, the question would read, 'that we send the executive committee to the Board of Supervisors and the County Planning Commission to express the need for a new park system.' Is there any discussion on the proposed amendment?" When the proposed amendment has been discussed and voted on, you return to the main question for further discussion.

It is also possible to amend an amendment, and although this may sound a little complicated at first, it is handled just like the above example. Keep these rules in mind:

1. The amendment to an amendment means just that! Do not accept a second amendment to the main question.

2. Vote on amendments in the reverse order of their proposal. That is: first, vote on the amendment to the amendment, second, vote on the amendment, and third, vote on the main question.

3. Every step opens up further discussion and possibly other subsidiary motions.

Motions That Require a Two-Thirds Vote

Parliamentary procedure is based upon democratic principles and a majority rule; therefore, a simple majority vote is the rule for most motions. Whenever the membership is considering a matter which would deny individuals the right to speak or which would suspend a procedural rule of the organization or interfere with a plan already adopted, a two-thirds vote is required. That is, one-third of the membership has the right, in these instances, to insist that it be heard! There are four such instances:

1. Voting immediately. (*Robert's* calls this "moving the previous question.") During discussion on any motion that is debatable, (see table on pages 146 and 147) a member may rise and say, "I move we vote on this motion immediately." After the motion has been seconded, the presiding officer brings this motion to a vote without any discussion whatever. "All those in favor, please stand (raise a hand); all those opposed, please stand (raise a hand)." After counting both and doing some quick arithmetic, "The motion to vote immediately passes by the vote 68 to 34; therefore, we shall vote the question immediately. All those in favor of the question under discussion, please say 'aye,'" etc., *or* "The motion to vote immediately is defeated by the vote 68 to 35; therefore, we will continue discussion of the question under discussion, which is . . . ."

2. Limiting or extending debate. A motion to limit debate is in order on any motion that is debatable (see table on pages 146 and 147). "I move to limit debate on this question to a *total time* of one hour," *or* "I move to limit the time of *each speaker* on this question to five minutes," *or* "I move that the time of the speaker be *extended* by 10 minutes." The presiding officer (after the second) follows with, "It has been moved that. . . . This motion is *not debatable,* but may be amended. Those in favor of the motion, please rise (pause); be seated. Those opposed to the motion, please rise (pause); be seated. The vote is 27 affirmative and 13 negative. Since there is a two-thirds affirmative vote, the motion is carried."

3. Objecting to the consideration of a question. Occasionally a member may want to avoid entirely discussion and decision on a main motion, resolution, or recommendation that he or she believes is embarrassing or inappropriate. The procedure is simple:

> **M:** "I move an objection to the consideration of this question."

AM: "I second this motion."

PO: *(since no discussion is in order)* "Objection has been moved to the consideration of this question. All in favor of considering the question, please rise (pause); be seated. Those opposed to considering the question, please rise (pause); be seated. The vote is 42 affirmative and 81 negative. Since the objection failed to receive a two-thirds negative vote, the question is now open for discussion." *(As always, you must state the vote in the affirmative and ask for the affirmative vote **before** the negative vote.)*

4. Suspending the rules. The standing rules of an organization sometimes interfere with desirable procedures which would facilitate business or accommodate a special situation. Setting a rule aside temporarily can provide this flexibility. This motion cannot, however, be applied to the constitution, bylaws, or to the organization's standard code of parliamentary procedure, *i.e., Robert's* or *Sturgis.*

M: "I move to suspend the rule requiring committee reports before business items so that we can elect a new secretary."

AM: "I second the motion."

PO: "It has been moved and seconded to suspend the rule that interferes with electing a secretary at this time. Those in favor, please rise (pause); be seated. Those opposed, please rise (pause); be seated. The vote is 51 affirmative and 19 negative. Since there is a two-thirds affirmative vote, the motion is carried. We will now proceed with the election of a secretary."

Rights and Privileges of Members

If it were not for parliamentary procedure, presiding officers could run a meeting just about any way they choose. In fact, some of them do, even with parliamentary procedure, especially when the membership is uninformed about its rights and privileges. The successful leader will not only honor membership rights and privileges but also inform members of them whenever possible and appropriate.

In addition to the right to discuss, to make motions, and to vote, members have the right to appeal decisions of the chair; to withdraw a motion presented; and to request action or information on urgent questions involving correct procedures for the immediate convenience, comfort, and safety of the membership, of another member, or of themselves. These rights and privileges are expressed in seven forms, and each of them can be expressed to the presiding officer without recognition and *except for an appeal from a decision of the chair none of them require a second.*

1. Appealing a Decision from the Presiding Officer

Even well-intentioned presiding officers sometimes make mistakes or act unfairly. Parliamentary procedure provides the membership with this method of sustaining or overruling a decision of the chair.

> **M:** "I appeal from the decision of the chair."
>
> **AM:** "I second the appeal," *or* "I second the motion."
>
> **PO:** "The decision of the chair has been appealed from." *(The presiding officer then states the reasons for the decision and the maker of the motion may state reasons for the appeal. After opportunity for discussion, the vote is taken – not on the appeal, but on sustaining or overruling the chair's decision.)* "Those in favor of sustaining the decision of the chair, say 'aye' (pause); those opposed to sustaining the decision of the chair say 'nay' (pause); the decision of the chair has been sustained (overruled)."

(It is possible, of course, that the chair will elect to change the decision or the member may drop the appeal any time during this process.)

2. Point of Order

This is an attempt to call to the attention of everyone present a violation of the rules, an omission or an error, and to get a ruling from the presiding officer.

M: "I rise to a point of order."

PO: "State your point of order."

M: "The vote just taken is out of order because there was no call for discussion before the vote."

PO: "Your point of order is well taken. The vote just taken is out of order. We will now discuss the motion just voted on. Will the secretary please read that motion." *(The secretary reads the motion.)* "Is there any discussion on the motion just read by the secretary? . . . ," etc.

3. Parliamentary Inquiry

M: "I rise to a parliamentary inquiry."

PO: "State your inquiry."

M: "Is a motion to recess in order at this time?"

PO: "It is."

4. Request for information

M: "I rise to a parliamentary inquiry."

PO: "State your inquiry."

M: "Do we have a quorum at this time?"

PO: "Will all voting members present please stand (pause); thank you. There are 27 voting members present. Twenty-five constitutes a quorum. Yes, we have a quorum at this time."

5. Permission to Ask a Question

M: "I rise to a parliamentary inquiry."

PO: "State your inquiry."

M: "May I ask the speaker a question?"

PO: *(directed to the speaking member)* "Ms. Beck, are you willing to answer a question at this time?"

AM: "I would prefer to conclude my prepared statement first."

PO: "The speaker will answer your question when she has concluded her prepared statement."

6. Withdrawing a Motion

A member presenting a motion "owns" it until it has been given to the membership by the presiding officer with the words "Is there any discussion?" For this reason the maker of a motion can withdraw it up to this moment without permission from anybody including the one who seconded the motion. When a motion has been given to the members, however, they "own it" and only they can approve withdrawal.

As long as a member "owns" the motion, it can be withdrawn simply by the member's saying, "I withdraw my motion." The presiding officer states, "The motion is withdrawn," and raps the gavel once. When the membership "owns" a motion, and the maker requests that it be withdrawn, you say, "Is there any objection to withdrawing this motion?" Seeing none, the motion is withdrawn *(one rap of gavel)*. If there is objection to withdrawal, say, "Those in favor of allowing _____ to withdraw this motion, please say 'aye' . . . ," etc. "The motion is carried (defeated) and _____'s motion is (is not) withdrawn." *(Rap gavel once.)*

7. Dividing a Question

Have you ever had to lead a discussion on a motion that has two independent parts? It can become pretty confusing! To keep things simple, it is best to divide these "double" motions into two separate main motions. For example:

> **M:** "I move that we raise the dues $1 and that we publish a weekly newsletter."
>
> **AM:** *(before or after the motion is seconded)* "I *request* that this motion be divided into two motions: (1) that we raise the dues $1 and (2) that we publish a weekly newsletter."
>
> **PO:** "This will be done. The motion now open for discussion is: that we raise the dues $1."

You should divide the double question yourself if it would clearly simplify the processing of business and no member has requested it. When you do this, however, always ask if there is any objection. If there is, listen to the objection and, if it is valid in your judgment, propose a revised version of your first proposal. If there continues to be some objection, bring it to a vote.

Division of the Assembly

Any member has the right to verify an indecisive voice or hand vote by requiring the voters to rise and be counted.

> **M:** *(without waiting for recognition)* "Division," *or* "I call for division."
>
> **PO:** "Division has been called for. Those in favor of the motion that . . . ," *(report the motion)* "please rise. The vice president will please count (pause); be seated. Those opposed to this motion, please rise (pause); the vote is 'yes,' 48, 'no,' 46. The motion is carried."

It is good practice for the presiding officer to take the initiative in calling for "division" whenever there is a close voice or hand vote, especially on important questions.

Summary

Harold H. Burton, Associate Justice of the Supreme Court of the United States has written:

> Parliamentary procedure is essential to competent self-government. It leads, as promptly, fairly, and intelligently as possible, to the discovery of common agreement. Free people will do well to learn it and use it in every policy-forming group, from a troop of scouts to the Parliament of Man.

Some leaders cower at the thought of parliamentary procedure and its complexities and avoid it at all costs. Others use it aggressively at the expense of basic rights and privileges of an intimidated membership.

Leaders who are successful in getting the membership involved in decision making and the work of carrying out those decisions when the meeting is over are the ones who practice the fundamentals of parliamentary law. These principles honor individual rights and obligations, full and free discussion of every issue, and a system of making decisions that everyone requires and can count on.

Finally, the key to effective parliamentary procedure is to keep it simple. Let every member know what is going on. Explain everyone's rights, privileges, and options. If you, yourself, are still a little shaky about all this, get yourself a copy of your favorite reference, *Robert's*, or *Sturgis*, and then study and practice what you've learned. Remember, no organization can be more effective and efficient in decision making than the level of competence of the presiding officer.

19

Formal Leadership Responsibilities

The formal business meeting, conducted according to the rules of parliamentary procedure, has a very important place in our social order and way of life. As an officer, you are more likely to be called upon to lead a meeting of this kind than any of the more informal types. While it differs from other kinds of meetings, many of the same rules for effective leadership apply. There are, however, the following differences, which affect your responsibility as leader or presiding officer.

1. Tradition has defined a well-established order of business which you should know and be able to follow.

2. You have far more powers (both expressed and implied) than does the leader of a less formal meeting.

3. The members of your group will be more or less familiar with the processes of parliamentary procedure and will be checking up on your work as a leader.

4. Deliberations result generally in formal recorded action: formal proposals are made, discussed, voted upon, and recorded.

5. Deliberations themselves, as well as the order of business, follow recognized rules of procedure.

Your first responsibility as a leader or presiding officer of a group of this kind, then, is to become familiar with the rules of the game, with parliamentary procedure. Hopefully, the preceding chapter has helped you along.

Knowing that all these rules exist, let us take a look at your job as a leader and what you should do to make such meetings run smoothly and function effectively.

Your major responsibilities as presiding officer of a formal meeting are these:

● *To initiate* items or proposals for the members to consider; to bring before them matters on which they may wish to take action.

● *To facilitate* the deliberations and actions of the group; to make it easier for the members to conduct the business which has brought them together.

● *To orient* and guide the members in the conduct of their business.

● *To encourage* and bring about a free and complete discussion of matters brought before the meeting and to act as a harmonizer when debate waxes a little too warm.

● *To finalize* the discussion by summarizing and bringing the question to a decision.

You will recognize these roles from the discussion in Chapter 2, and you should emphasize that the formal business meeting is also built around the democratic process and utilizes it in group discussion.

Let us take these five responsibilities and discuss how you might discharge them in order that your meeting will function as it should.

1. Initiate. Bringing up matters to be considered in the meeting is a responsibility which you share with the other members of the group, but be prepared to do more than your share. This calls for a little preliminary planning on your part. It might be well for you to meet with the other officers as an executive committee, and especially with the secretary, to make preliminary plans for the meeting, anticipate items which may be brought up from the floor for action, go over the minutes of the previous meeting to determine whether or not there is any unfinished business, and list items which the officers may wish to have considered. (A brief meeting of this kind, the day before your larger group meets, will enable you to think through and prepare for at least some of the matters to be considered.)

As you consider the order of business of a formal meeting, many other instances will be found where it will be appropriate for you, as presiding officer, to initiate matters. The accepted order of business is as follows:

> Call to order
> Introduction of guests
> Reading of minutes of previous meeting
> Treasurer's report
> Reports of standing committees
> Reports of special committees
> Old business
> New business
> Program
> Adjournment

After calling the meeting to order, initiate discussion, or at least set the stage for questions and discussion. For example: let's assume you have called for reports of standing committees, and the program committee has made its report. You, as chairperson, might say, "Thank you. You have heard the report of the program committee. Are there any questions about it?" (Pause) "If not, what is your pleasure concerning it?"

Note that you have given your group an opportunity (by means of the two questions you raised) to get to work. Twice you've tossed the ball and given the members a chance to take over.

You can initiate action by the members by asking such questions as:

> Is there any discussion?
> Are there any questions?
> Is there any unfinished business to come before us?
> What is your pleasure concerning this report?

2. *Facilitate.* This is your most important responsibility. A well-known entertainer was once characterized in these words, "She

is the kind of person who can make a 90-minute meeting seem to last a whole hour and a half." At best, formal business meetings are not too interesting to some members, who may get a little impatient to get business out of the way and move on to the program and the eats. So it behooves you, as the presiding officer, to try to make that 90-minute business session seem like only an hour, *not* like an hour and a half. It can be done, too, if you do your part smoothly. Here's how:

a. Know your parliamentary procedure. Review Chapter 18; then if you need to, get either *Sturgis* or *Robert's* and study up so that you know what you're supposed to do and say so well that it becomes second nature.

b. Use a parliamentarian. Even though you know your stuff, it's always best to have someone readily available to clarify the difficult questions. Appoint a parliamentarian and have him or her on call with the book of rules to help you out of the tangles which can befall even an experienced presiding officer.

c. Keep things moving. When you've given the group a decent interval in which to respond after asking a question, pass on to the next order of business. Develop a sense of timing and use it.

d. Avoid making long explanations or speeches. Your job isn't to give facts; it's to initiate and to facilitate. Above all, don't take the chance of insulting the members' intellegence by a lengthy explanation of something which may be and probably is just as well understood by them as by you. If you do have to play the role of fact-giver, you should be the *last* source of information—literally and chronologically, last. If you have something to say for or against a motion and feel strongly enough about it so that you *must* speak, ask the vice president to take the chair and serve until the motion has been disposed of. Don't do it as presiding officer.

e. Use your secretary. Brief this valuable officer on items of unfinished business from the minutes of the last meeting. Condition your secretary to get the motions down on paper as they are made, and prepare him or her to read them off quickly and clearly when called upon to do so.

f. Keep your eyes open. Be alert and watch the members all the time. Don't keep your gaze fixed on any one person or portion of the room, and don't let your eyes stray to the ceiling or to the windows. Always be on the lookout for members who wish to have the floor, and be quick to recognize them.

g. Use the authority that you have as presiding officer. Use it appropriately, of course, but use it. No one can speak without recognition from you, and you decide and state whether a motion has passed or has been defeated. Don't hesitate. Keep things moving. That gavel was given you for a purpose, so use it whenever you make a decision or call for order.

h. Appreciate and use the procedure of handling business by general consent where appropriate. If a matter under discussion obviously has the unanimous approval of all the members, don't go through the process of asking for a motion, a second, and a vote, but bring the matter to a close by a statement such as this: "It seems to be the consensus that we do . . . , and if there are no objections, it is so ordered." The approving of the minutes of the previous meeting, for example, is generally handled in this manner by general consent when the presiding officer states, "You have heard the minutes of the previous meeting. Are there any additions or corrections?" (Pause) "If not, they stand approved as read." The reports of standing committees may be handled in much the same manner. (This technique is an important time saver, so be on the alert for situations where it may be applied.)

The use of all these procedures will do much to facilitate the conduct of business by the group. Study them and practice them. Maybe you won't be able to make a 90-minute meeting seem only an hour long, but at least it won't seem any longer than an hour and a half.

3. Orient and guide. Let your members know what's going on.

a. What is the motion being discussed? When the discussion gets a little lengthy, redundant, or irrelevant, you should repeat the motion before continuing with discussion.

b. What vote is needed? Some require a simple majority, others two-thirds. You are expected to know, and you should inform the members in advance of calling for their vote.

c. What alternatives do the members have? Frequently during debate it is possible to sense a member's desire to limit debate, amend the motion being discussed, or refer the question to a committee. In many organizations members are not totally aware of their various procedural alternatives. Tell them, even help them with the proper wording of the action they seem to want.

4. Encourage free discussion. While it seems to be a fairly common practice for a group to discuss a matter before a motion is made and seconded, this is not the correct procedure in a formal business meeting. A motion should be made and seconded in order to start discussion, and a member may make a motion or second it, *not* necessarily because he or she favors it, but *to have it discussed.* Similarly, as presiding officer, when someone begins to discuss a matter without its being brought on the floor as a motion, you should ask that it be stated in the form of a motion so that it may be discussed. Therefore, be ready with the question, "Do you wish to state that in the form of a motion, Mr. White?," *or* "Will you please put that in the form of a motion?" Then ask for a second, and the matter is ready to be discussed.

In conducting the discussion of a motion, make every effort to keep the discussion balanced. Give the person who made the motion the first chance to discuss it. Then try to get someone to present an opposite point of view to that of the first speaker. Alternating speakers for and against the motion will serve to bring out most of the facts which should be considered and will make for higher quality decisions. Another good rule to follow is to make sure that every member has a chance to speak at least once on a motion before any member is permitted to speak twice.

If a really difficult problem is under consideration, make use of the buzz session as described in Chapter 9. Very often persons who would be too timid to call for the floor and speak on the proposition under discussion will have no inhibitions about discussing it freely in a small group. This technique is rarely used, but it is a good one when the group is large, when the problem requires free and complete discussion, and when immediate action is preferable to referring the problem to a committee.

To break up into buzz groups, simply ask for a motion that "we discuss this problem informally in small groups"; have it seconded, then discussed, and brought to a vote. After a specified time, ask each group to give a report on its conclusions, and the meeting will resume its identity as a formal meeting. This procedure is not very well-known, but it is one of the best in arriving at an answer to a difficult situation which must or should be settled immediately. It is surprising how an informal discussion will bring out worthwhile suggestions when the more formal procedure of the larger group fails to do so. Try it the next time your group has a problem of this kind.

5. *Finalize.* In the interest of keeping things moving as well as taking effective action, you must be prepared to summarize discussion and bring the group to a decision. Sometimes action may be taken by general consent, as described earlier in this chapter. In this case, you would simply summarize the discussion briefly, state that it seems to be agreed that certain action should be taken, ask if there is any objection, and if there is none, say that it is so ordered. If there is objection, it must be voted upon. Before calling for a vote, you should restate the motion (have the secretary read it if it is long and involved), ask "Are you ready for the question?," and then put it to a vote.

Your business meetings will be more than just successful when you have made these five functions a part of your personal leadership style. Not only will you have moved business along at a challenging pace with lots of member participation and high quality decisions, you will be rewarded with an awareness of group achievement and membership satisfaction.

20

Strategy for Change

A leader is an initiator, constantly looking ahead, sensing the need for change, and bringing proposals involving change to colleagues or clientele. Many persons, by virtue of their professional positions, are continually faced with the problem of how to present proposals for changes of policy, of procedure, and of practice. Their problem is not just one of how to present these proposals, but one of how to present them in such a way that people will accept, approve, and take action on them. The leader in civic and public affairs is faced with similar tasks.

This responsibility is not limited to those in the top echelons of administrative authority or to the elected leaders of any group, for the role of initiator is not limited to leadership alone; it must be played by many if there is to be real progress. Thus, the teacher who needs a piece of new equipment for his or her laboratory; the department head who wants an increased budget for the department; any member of the organization or group who feels that a change is needed in policy or method is faced with the same problem—that of presenting a proposal or request in such a way that it may be adopted.

This is the last and perhaps the most difficult and complex of the leadership skills to be discussed. In contrast to skill in making explanations, where the end product was that of developing understanding, here you must secure understanding plus positive action *which involves change.*

Most of us seem to resist change. We find it easier and more comfortable to follow the familiar or routine way of doing things than to venture down new and untried paths. Sometimes, even when we become convinced of the value or even the necessity of change, we resist it.

Just why do people resist change? What are the things which block it? What are the attitudes, the feelings that obstruct and prevent acceptance of change? The following are some of the reasons why it is often so difficult to gain acceptance of a new idea, a new policy, or a new program.

1. Fear. Fear of the unknown; fear of the consequences; fear that the change may affect us adversely.

2. Distrust. Distrust of the motives behind the proposed change; distrust and fear of the motives of the one proposing the change.

3. Lack of understanding. We dislike ambiguous situations. We like to know where we stand. We are comfortable in the old familiar way of doing things, and it is difficult for us to see our place in the new order. When we have not had the opportunity to participate in planning the change, we do not have as complete an understanding of it as the proponent or proponents of the new proposal do.

4. Aversion to being considered "different." We resist change when it requires us to be different—different from our colleagues, from our associates. We resist change when it involves a procedure radically different from that followed by other similar organizations and groups.

These are some of the major factors which block change. Perhaps these may be summed up: **all of us have the urge to protect and preserve that which we now have.**

Some of the other factors which should be considered when we attempt to implement change are:

● That older people are less receptive to change, generally, than younger persons are.

● That educated persons tend to be more receptive than those with less education; that the educated person may be swayed more by reason—by facts—while those with less education may be governed more by their emotions.

● That persons who have taken a public stand on an issue are less prone to change than those who have not.

● That we may accept milder changes more readily than radical ones; and gradual changes more readily than abrupt ones.

● That we tend to identify the change with the person who is proposing it. If we believe in and trust that individual personally, we tend to accept the proposal; if we fear or distrust the individual, we transfer this same attitude to the change being proposed.

Thus, it is easy to see why gaining acceptance of change is so difficult and why proposals for change must be so *carefully thought through and presented.*

What follows is an outline which may be of value in planning and presenting proposals for change:

Presentation	**Purpose**

I. INTRODUCTION

1. Express appreciation for privilege of presenting proposal.

2. Give short historical background to and show need for proposal.

3. State and stress objective of change and secure approval of this objective.

1. To gain attention, create interest, and set a friendly atmosphere for the program.

2. To make a favorable first impression of you, your motives, and your objectives.

3. To lay a foundation for your proposal.

II. STATEMENT OF PROPOSAL

1. Relate proposal to objective.

2. Present all pertinent facts and data.

3. Use appropriate visual aids.

1. To develop understanding; to make it entirely clear just what you are requesting.

III. DISCUSSION

1. Present arguments both for and against proposal.

2. Refute arguments opposing it and show that they are unimportant.

3. Present alternative proposal if opposition obviously is too strong.

1. To show that the proposal has been considered thoroughly.

2. To show that evidence supporting it far outweighs arguments against it.

3. To anticipate and answer questions concerning it.

IV. CONCLUSION

1. Summarize and emphasize main points supporting proposal.

2. Request consideration and favorable action.

1. To leave audience with a summation of the important supporting evidence in favor of the proposal.

2. To gain sympathy for the request and encourage favorable action.

It should be emphasized that even though you plan your presentation according to this outline and attempt to follow it, you will seldom be allowed to do so completely. There will be questions raised and comments made which will cause you to deviate from your set plan. It may well be said that such a plan is only a point of departure and is made "to deviate from." However, to make such a plan will help you to think through your proposal and will enable you to support it more intelligently under fire.

Regardless of whether or not you follow the suggested plan, there are certain key points which should be observed in your presentation.

1. Your motives and the objectives of your proposal must be unassailable and unquestionable. It must be made clear to your audience from the outset that the proposal is true and that it must be accepted. Otherwise, your plan is doomed for failure.

2. Present the facts and arguments both for and against your request, especially if you anticipate resistance and objections. Doing so will serve to allay any fears that you may not have considered all aspects and consequences of your project. If, however, you feel that your audience is friendly and already disposed toward it, present only the arguments for your proposal.

3. Present the strongest arguments supporting your proposal last. Start with the weaker and less important evidence favorable to your plan; follow with any arguments against it; finish with a refutation of opposing evidence; and, with your strongest arguments, support it. Last impressions are likely to be more lasting.

4. Assemble and have all the facts and data concerning your proposal with you.

5. Make your proposal explicit and specific. Remember that all of us dislike ambiguous situations and generally want to know exactly what is involved before accepting.

6. Prepare, assemble, and use appropriate visual aids—charts, pictures, maps, catalogs, diagrams—whatever will contribute to understanding.

7. Gear your presentation to all persons in your audience; take into consideration their known characteristics, attitudes, opinions, age, maturity, level of education, and whether or not they may have taken a public stand on your proposal.

8. Check and recheck the major reasons why people resist change. Make certain that your presentation is calculated to remove these blocks.

9. Close with an appeal for a sympathetic consideration of your request and for appropriate action.

10. If it is likely that you will experience serious unshakable objections to your proposal, be prepared to submit alternative courses of action.

If, for example, the group obviously feels that the change involved is too great to be effected at once, ask for approval of parts of it—the preliminary steps, perhaps. If the members appear to fear the consequences of such a change, suggest that it be tried experimentally in a limited way before final and complete adoption.

If they agree that a change seems to be in order and that the objectives and general idea of your proposal are acceptable, but they still object to certain details, ask for approval of your proposal in principle and for their suggestions regarding the details.

Do not be discouraged if you fail. The mere fact that they have listened to you, that you have had an opportunity to present your thoughts, may bring favorable action later, when they have had time to think over your proposal.

Consider the effort to have been a victory, if, at some later date, your proposal (or a portion of it) is adopted through the leadership of someone else (especially the boss).

Index